THE WISDOM OF LOVE

IN THE SERVICE OF LOVE

THE WISDOM OF LOVE IN
THE SERVICE OF LOVE

Emmanuel Levinas on Justice, Peace, and Human Rights

Roger Burggraeve

Preface by David A. Boileau
Translation and Concluding Essay by Jeffrey Bloechl

MARQUETTE
UNIVERSITY

PRESS

Marquette Studies in Philosophy

No. 29

Andrew Tallon, Series Editor

LIBRARY OF CONGRESS CATALOGING-IN-PUBLICATION DATA

Burggraeve, Roger, 1942-
  [Levinas over vrede en mensenrechten. English]
  The wisdom of love in the service of love : Emmanuel Levinas on justice, peace, and human rights / Roger Burggraeve ; preface by David A. Boileau ; translation and concluding essay by Jeffrey Bloechl.
      p. cm. — (Marquette studies in philosophy ; no. 29)
  Includes bibliographical references and index.
  ISBN 0-87462-652-8
  1. Levinas, Emmanuel—Ethics. I. Title. II. Marquette studies in philosophy ; #29.
  B2430.L484 .B866 2002
  170'.92—dc21

                        2002014544

The series editor would like to thank Didier Pollefeyt,
of the Faculty of Theology, Leuven University,
for his great help in furnishing the two photos for the covers.

MARQUETTE UNIVERSITY PRESS
MILWAUKEE

The Association of Jesuit University Presses

TABLE OF CONTENTS

Abbreviations of Works By Levinas

AE: *Autrement qu'être ou au-delà de l'essence*, La Haye: Martinus Nijhoff 1974. [English translation (ET): *Otherwise than Being or Beyond Essence*, trans. A. Lingis. The Hague, Martinus Nijhoff 1981.]

AEG: "Anlits und erste Gewalt. Ein Gespräch über Phänomenologie und Ethik" (interview with M.J. Lenger), in *Spuren in Kunst und Gesellschaft* (1987), no. 20: 29-34.

AR: "Amour et révélation," in P. Huot-Pleuroux, et.al., *La charité aujourd'hui*, Paris: Editions S.O.S. 1981, pp. 133-148.

AS: *Autrement que savoir* (interventions in discussions following contributions by G. Petitdemange and J. Rolland on the thought of Levinas), Paris: Osiris 1988, pp. 27-29, 32-34, 59-62, 67-95.

AT: *Alterité et transcendence* (Textes réunis et présentés par P. Hayat), Montpellier: Fata Morgana 1995.

AV: *L'au-delà du verset. Lectures et discours talmudiques*, Paris: Minuit 1982. [ET: *Beyond the Verse. Talmudic Readings and Lectures*, translated by G.D. Mole. Bloomington and Indianapolis: Indiana University Press 1996.]

BPW: *Emmanuel Levinas. Basic Philosophical Writings*, edited by A.T. Peperzak, S. Critchley and R. Bernasconi. Bloomington and Indianapolis: Indiana University Press 1996.

CCH: "Comme un consentement à l'horrible," in *Le Nouvel Observateur* (1988), no. 1211: 82-83.

CI: "Crime et inhumanité" (recorded by F. Poirié), in *Les Dossiers de Globe* (1987), no. 1: 21.

CJ-I: Intervention in *La conscience juive. Données et débats*, Paris: 1963, p. 31.

CPP: *Collected Philosophical Papers*, translated by A. Lingis. The Hague: Nijhoff (Kluwer) 1987.

CV: "De la conscience à la veille. A partir de Husserl," in *Bijdragen* 34(1974), n. 3-4, July-December: 285-287. Also taken up in **DVI**, pp. 34-61.

CVH: "The Contemporary Criticism of the Idea of Value and the Prospects for Humanism," in E.A. Maziarz (ed.), *Value and Values in Evolution*, New York: Gordon and Beach 1979, pp. 179-188.

DAH: "Les droits de l'homme," in COMMISSION NATIONALE DES DROITS DE L'HOMME (ed.), *Les droits de l'homme en questions*, Paris La Documentation Française 1988, pp. 43-45.

DEHH: *En découvrant l'existence avec Husserl et Heidegger*, Paris: Vrin 1949 (1st edition); 1967 (2nd expanded edition with "Essais nouveaux") (we refer to the second edition).
[ET (partial): *Discovering Existence with Husserl*, translated by R. Cohen. Bloomington and Indianapolis: Indiana University Press 1988.]

DHBV: "Droits de l'homme et bonne volonté," in *Le supplément* (1989), no. 168: 57-60. Also taken up in **EN**, pp. 231-235.

DHDA: "Les droits de l'homme et les droits d'autrui," in M. Borghi, et.al., *L'indivisibilité des droits de l'homme*, Fribourg: 1985, pp. 35-45.

DL: *Difficile liberté. Essais sur le judaïsme*, Paris: Albin Michel 1963 (1st edition); 1976 (revised and expanded edition) (we refer to the second edition).
[ET: *Difficult Freedom. Essays on Judaism*, translated by S. Hand. London: Athlone 1990.]

DMT:*Dieu, la Mort et le Temps*, Paris: Grasset 1993. Also includes *La mort et le temps*, Paris: L'Herne 1991.

DVI: *De Dieu qui vient à l'idée* (Essais), Paris: Vrin 1982.
[ET: *Of God Who Comes to Mind*, translated by B. Bergo. Palo Alto: Stanford University Press 1998].

EE: *De l'existence à l'existant*, Paris: Fontaine-Vrin 1947 (1st edition); Paris: Vrin 1978 (2nd edition with "Préface à la deuxième édition").
[ET: *Existence and Existents*, translated by A. Lingis. The Hague: Martinus Nijhoff 1978. Part of the introduction and Chapter 3, section 2, also translated by A. Lingis and taken up in **LR**, pp. 30-36].

EFP:"Entretiens Emmanuel Levinas–François Poirié," in F. Poirié, *Emmanuel Levinas. Qui êtes-vous?*, Lyon: La Manufacture 1987, pp. 62-136.

EI: *Ethique et infini. Dialogues avec Philippe Nemo*, Paris: Fayard-Radio France 1982.
[*Ethics and Infinity. Conversations with Philippe Nemo*, translated by R. Cohen. Pittsburgh: Duquesne University Press 1985].

EL: *Emmanuel Levinas* (texts by and on Levinas, collected by C. Chalier and M. Abensour), Paris:L'Herne 1991.

EN: *Entre Nous. Essais sur la pensée-à-l'autre*, Paris: Grasset 1991.

EP: "Enigme et phénomène," in *Esprit* 33(1965), no. 6, June: 1128-1142. Also taken up in **DEHH** (1967), pp. 203-217.
[ET: "Enigma and Phenomena, in **CPP**, pp. 61-74.]

EPP: "Ethique et philosophie première. La proximité de l'autre" (interview with A.-C. Benchelah), in *Phréatique* (1986) no. 39: 121-127.

ESC: "Exteriority as the Source of Civilization" (in collaboration with R. Burggraeve), in B. Bremer (rd.), *Europe by Nature. Starting-Points for a Sustainable Development*, Amsterdam-Assen- Maastricht: Conspectus Europae-Van Gorcum 1992, pp. 2905-2921.

EVA: "De l'Evasion," in *Recherches philosophiques* 5(1935-1936): 373-392. Published in book form, introduced and annotated by J. Rolland, as *De l'Evasion*, Montpellier: Fata Morgana 1982.

FHP: "Fribourg, Husserl et la phénoménologie," in *Revue d'Allemagne et des pays de languae allemande* 5(1931), no. 43, 15 May: 402-414. Also taken up in **IH**, pp. 94-106.

HAH: *Humanisme de l'autre homme*, Montpellier: Fata Morgana 1972.
[ET: The three essays, all translated by A. Lingis, are taken up in **CPP**, respectively "Meaning and Sense" at pp. 75-107, "Humanism and Anarchy" at 127-139, and "No Identity" at pp. 141- 151].

HN: *A l'heure des nations* (Lectures talmudiques, essais et entretiens), Paris: Minuit 1988.
[ET: *In the Time of the Nations*, translated by M.B. Smith. Bloomington and Indianapolis: Indiana University Press 1994.]

HS: *Hors sujet. Essais*, Montpellier: Fata Morgana 1987.
[ET: *Outside the Subject*, translated by M.B. Smith. Bloomington and Indianapolis: Indiana University Press 1994.]

I: "Ideology and Idealism," in M. Fox (ed.), *Modern Jewish Ethics. Theory and Practice*, Ohio State University Press 1975, pp. 121-138. Also in **LR**, pp. 235-248.

ID: "A l'image de Dieu d'après Rabbi Haim Volozhiner," in H.J. Adriaanse, et.al., *God, goed, en kwaad*, 's-Gravenhage: Boekencentrum 1977, pp. 254-275. Also taken up in **AV**, pp. 182-200.

IEP "Israël: éthique et politique" (interview by S. Malka with E. Levinas and A. Finkielkraut), in *Les nouveaux cahiers* (1982-1983), no. 71: 1-8.

IH: *Les imprévus de l'histoire* (Essais) (Textes réunis et présentés par P. Hayat), Montpellier: Fata Morgana 1994.

II: *L'Intrigue de l'Infini* (Textes réunis et présentés par M.-A. Lescourret), Paris: Flammarion 1994.

IM: "Intentionalité et métaphysique," in *Revue philosophique de la France et de l'Etranger*, vol. 149, 1959, no. 4, October-December: 471-479. Also taken up in **DEHH** (1967), pp. 137-144.

IRDH: "Interdit de la représentation et 'droits de l'homme'," in A. Rassial and J.J. Rassial (eds.), *L'interdit de la représentation*, Paris: Seuil 1984, pp. 107-113.

IS: "Intentionalité et sensation," in *Revue internationale de philosophie* 19(1965), nos. 71-72, fasc. 1-2: 34-54. Also taken up in **DEHH** (1967), pp. 144-162.

JG: "Jacob Gordin," in *Les nouveaux cahiers* (1972-1973), no. 31: 20-22.

JK: Judaïsme et kénose," in *Archivio di Filosofia* 53(1985), vol. 2, nos. 2-3, Padova: CEDAM, pp.13-28. Also taken up in **HN**, pp. 133-151.

JR: "Judaïsme et révolution," in *Jeunesse et révolution dans la conscience juive*, Paris: 1972, pp. 3-12.

LAV: "'L'au-delà du verset.' Un entretien avec Emmanuel Levinas (à propos de Mère Teresa)," in L. Balbont, *Mère Teresa en notre âme et conscience*, Paris: Seuil 1982, pp. 111-112.

LC: "Liberté et commandement," in *Revue de métaphysique et de morale* 58(1953): 264-272. Republished in book form, with foreword by P. Hayat, as *Liberté et commandement*, Montpellier: Fata Morgana 1994; includes the essay "Transcendence et hauteur," originally published in *Bulletin de la Société française de philosophie* 56(1962), no. 3: 89-113, with discussion and correspondence. [ET: "Freedom and Command," translated by A. Lingis, in **CPP**, pp. 15-23; "Transcendence and Height," translated by T. Chanter, S. Critchley, N. Walker, A. Peperzak, in **BPW**, pp. 11-31, 172-173 (with discussion and correspondence)]

LPI: "La laïcité et la pensée d'Israël," in *La laïcité*, Paris: Presses Universitaires de France 1960, pp.45-58.

LR: *The Levinas Reader*, edited by S. Hand. Oxford: Blackwell 1989.

MB: *Sur Maurice Blanchot* (Essais), Montpellier: Fata Morgana 1975.

MC: E. Husserl, *Méditations cartésiennes. Introduction à la phénoménologie* (translated from the German by G. Pfeiffer and E. Levinas), Paris: Colin 1931 (1st edition); republished by Paris: Vrin 1947, 1953, 1969.

MBJC: "La pensée de Martin Buber et le judaïsme contemporain," in *Martin Buber. L'homme et le philosophie*, Bruxelles: Editions de l'Institut de Sociologie de l'Université Libre de Bruxelles 1968, pp. 43-58.

MPR: "La mémoire d'un passé non révolu" (interview with F. Ringelheim), in *Revue de l'Université de Bruxelles* (1987), no. 1-2: 11-20.

MT: "Le moi et la totalité," in *Revue de métaphysique et de morale* 59(1954), no. 4, October- December: 353-373. Also taken up in EN, pp. 25-52.
[ET: "The Ego and the Totality," translated by A. Lingis in CPP, pp. 25-45.]

ND: "Le nom de Dieu d'après quelques textes talmudiques. Discussion," in *Débats sur le langage théologique*, Paris: Aubier-Montaigne 1969, pp. 53-70. The discussion (and not the essay itself) is also taken up in II, pp. 219-240.

NLT: *Nouvelles lectures talmudiques*, Paris: Minuit 1996.

NP *Noms Propres* (Essais), Montpellier: Fata Morgana 1976.

P: "Préface," in S. Mosès, *Système et révélation. La philosophie de Franz Rosenzweig*, Paris: Seuil 1982. Also taken up in HN, pp. 175-185.

PA: "De phénoménologie à l'éthique" (interview with Levinas by R. Kearney), in *Esprit*, no. 234 (1997), no. 7, July: 121-140 (translated from English into French by A. Bernard-Kearney; original publication in R. Kearney (ed.), *States of Mind. Dialogue with Contemporary Thinkers on the European Mind*, Manchester: Manchester University Press 1995.

PIF: "La philosophie et l'idée de l'Infini," in *Revue de métaphysique et de morale* 62(1957), no. 3, July-September: 241-253. Also taken up in DEHH (1967), pp. 165-178.
[ET: "Philosophy and the Idea of Infinity," in A. Peperzak, *To the Other. Introduction to the Philosophy of Emmanuel Levinas*, West Lafayette: Purdue University Press 1993, pp. 88-119.]

PM: "The Paradox of Morality (interview with T. Wright, P. Hughes, A. Anley), trans. A. Benjamin and T. Wright in R. Bernasconi and D. Wood (eds.), *The Provocation of Levinas. Rethinking the Other*, London: Routledge 1988, pp. 168-180.

PP: "Paix et proximité," in *Les cahiers de la nuit surveillée*, no. 3, Lagrasse: 1984, pp. 339-346. Also taken up in TA, pp. 138-150.
[ET: "Peace and Proximity," translated by P. Atterton and S. Critchley, in BPW, pp. 161-169, 193-194.]

PPR: "The Primacy of Pure Practical Reason," translated by B. Billings, in *Man and World* 27(1994): 445-453.

QLT: *Quatre lectures talmudiques*, Paris: Minuit 1968.
[ET in E. Levinas, *Nine Talmudic Readings*, translated by A. Aronowicz. Bloomington and Indianapolis: Indiana University Press 1990, pp. 1-88, entitled "Four Talmudic Readings."]

RA: "Entretien" (recorded by L. Adert and J.-C. Aeschliemann), in J.-C. Aeschliemann (ed.), *Répondre d'autrui*, Neuchâtel: Baconnière 1989, pp. 9-16.

RR: "La ruine de la réprésentation," in the collection *Edmund Husserl 1859-1959*, La Haye: Nijhoff1959, pp. 73-85. Also taken up in **DEHH** (1967), pp. 125-135.

RTP: "Réflexions sur la 'technique' phénoménologique," in the collection *Husserl*, Paris: Minuit 1959, pp. 95-109. Also taken up in **DEHH** (1967), pp. 111-123.

SA: "Socialité et l'argent," in *25 années groupement Belge des Banques d'Epargne: 1961-1986. Allocutions Séance Académique*, Bruxelles: Groupement Belge des Banques d'Epargne 1987,pp. 13-19. Also taken up in R. Burggraeve, *Emmanuel Levinas et la socialité de l'argent. Un philosophie en quête de la réalité journalière. La genèse de 'Socalité et argent' ou l'ambiguïté de l'argent*, Leuven: Peeters 1997, pp. 79-85.

SaS: *Du sacré au saint. Cinq nouvelles lectures talmudiques*, Paris: Minuit 1977.
[ET in E. Levinas, *Nine Talmudic Readings*, translated by A. Aronowicz. Bloomington and Indianapolis: Indiana University Press 1990, pp. 89-197, entitled "From the Sacred to the Holy. Five New Talmudic Readings."]

SI: "La souffrance inutile," in *Las cahiers de la nuit surveillée*, no. 3, Lagrasse: 1984, pp. 329-338. Also taken up in **EN**, pp. 107-119.
[ET: "Useless Suffering," translated by R. Cohen in R. Bernasconi and D. Wood (eds.), *The Provocation of Levinas. Re-Thinking the Other*, London-New York: Routledge 1988, pp. 156- 169.]

TA: "Le temps et l'autre," 1st edition in the collection J. Wahl, et.al., *Le choix, le monde, l'existence*, Grenoble-Paris: Arthaud 1947, pp. 125-196; second edition in separate book form and with "Préface à deuxième édition," *Le temps et l'autre*, Montpellier: Fata Morgana 1979.
[ET: *Time and the Other*, translated by R. Cohen. Pittsburgh: Duquesne University Press 1987.]

TI: *Totalité et Infini*, La Haye: Nijhoff 1961 (first edition).
[ET: *Totality and Infinity*, translated by A. Lingis, The Hague: Martinus Nijhoff 1969.]

TIPH: *La théorie de l'intuition dans la phénoménologie de Husserl*, Paris: Alcan 1930 (1st edition); republished by Paris: Vrin 1963, 1970.
[ET: *The Theory of Intuition in Husserl's Phenomenology*, translated by A. Orianne. Evanston: Northwestern University Press 1973.]

TMD:"Temps messianiques (Discussion)," in *La conscience juive. Données et débats*, Paris: Presses Universitaires de France 1963, pp. 286-291.

TMI: "Temps messianiques (Introduction)," in *La conscience juive. Données et débats*, Paris: Presses Universitaires de France 1963, pp. 268-269.

TrI: *Transcendence et intelligibilité. Suivi d'un entretien*, Genève: Labor et Fides 1984. Also taken up (without discussion) in **II**, pp. 273-286.
[ET: "Transcendence and Intelligibility," translated by S. Critchley and T. Wright, in **BPW**, pp. 149-159, 191-193.]

U "De l'unicité," in *Archivio di Filosofia* 54 (1986), no. 1-3: 301-307. Also taken up in **EN**, pp. 209-217.

VA "La vocation de l'autre" (interview with E. Hirsch), in E. Hirsch (ed.), *Racismes. L'autre et son visage*, Paris: Cerf 1988, pp. 89-102.

WZE "Wat men van zichzelf eist, eist men van een heilige" (interview with J.F. Goud), in *Ter herkenning* 11 (1983), no. 5: 147-154.

Levinas Bibliography

For more extensive bibliographical information on publications by and on Levinas, see R. Burggraeve, *Emmanuel Levinas. Une bibliographie primaire et secondaire (1929-1985) avec complément (1985-1989)*, Leuven: Peeters 1990, 220 pp.

PREFACE

Through the scholarship of Roger Burggraeve, professor of moral theology at the Catholic University of Louvain (Flemish campus), the social and religious writings of Emmanuel Levinas are attracting the increased attention of the English-speaking world that they so richly deserve. A student and close friend of Levinas, Professor Burggraeve wrote his doctoral thesis on Levinas' thought and defended it in 1980; since then he has focussed a considerable portion of his scholarly efforts on understanding and interpreting the works of Levinas. Professor Burggraeve's excellent little book *From Self-Development to Solidarity: An Ethical Reading of Human Desire in its socio-Political Relevance According to Emmanuel Levinas* appeared in 1985, and has been followed by numerous articles; his extensive bibliographical survey of works by and about Levinas was published in 1990, and places us forever in his debt.

This fine translation from the Dutch by Jeffrey Bloechl brings the work of Professor Burggraeve once again into the English-speaking world. We can now share his close association with Levinas, his painstaking scholarship, and even though Burggraeve concentrates on Levinas' thought, also catch glimpses of a fine moral theologian in his own right. His book would make an excellent text for any ethics or theology course.

As we have known from other sources, the ethics of the French-Jewish philosopher Emmanuel Levinas (1905-1995) begins with the epiphany of the "face" of the other. At the same time in his first major work, *Totalité et Infini* (1961), he affirms that the other is invisible, in the sense that the face is irreducible to its phenomenality or appearance. This paradox of the epiphany as the invisibility of the other reveals the ethical meaning of the face expressed as the daily possibility of violence and as the prohibition of violence. Thus, for Levinas, ethics realizes itself as a "retaining" (*une retenue*), or a kind of aloofness of the

"I"—namely, a not doing what could indeed be done. The face of the other is the discrete but imperative word that affects me and appeals to me neither to use force nor to misuse, violate, totalize, hate or destroy the other: "thou shalt not kill." This first reservation or shame of the "I" about its own being, or its "*conatus essendi*," expresses itself positively in a heteronomous responsibility "through and for the other" (*par et pour autrui*). Levinas calls this responsibility "goodness," which is neither naive or trivial, but rather the difficult struggle, never with obvious victory, to overcome racism and antisemitism, the most extreme forms of moral evil. In his second major work, *Otherwise than Being or Beyond Essence* (1974), Levinas considers it the "wisdom of love" to discern this "goodness," and he argues that this wisdom implies an "extra-ordinary" way of "being-towards-God" (*être-à-Dieu*), as the Infinite and the "Good beyond Being."

With this book, Burggraeve brings together the social and political thought of Levinas—previously little-known and in large part unpublished, certainly in English—thus offering an uncommonly comprehensive introduction to the full breadth and profundity of Levinas' work. Burggraeve leads us through the development of Levinas' thought beyond the positions of Husserl and Heidegger, helping us to appreciate more fully the way Levinas transcends the atheistic or, more precisely, agnostic presuppositions of phenomenology, permitting us to better incorporate it into our own ethical and theological discourses. Levinas' major works provide only scattered clues about his position on these key issues; Jeffrey Bloechl is therefore certainly right to underline, in his concluding essay to this volume, the importance of Burggraeve's effort already to gather and order the diverse group of texts in play here, let alone comment on them and apply them. What all of that research brings to the center in Burggraeve's reading of Levinas is the proper definition of the good act itself, the taking up of responsibility and care for one's neighbor, both as inspired by a wisdom which is in the first instance biblical and as exercised in a situation which is at once ethical, social and political.

Emmanuel Levinas' original ethical metaphysics, so often and so easily misunderstood, is masterfully elucidated here by Professor Burggraeve. In Levinas, the ethics of self-fulfillment is transcended by an ethics of responsibility, especially through concepts like "substitution" (accepting care for the other all the way to accepting his or her very responsibility) and universal "solidarity." Each of us is responsible for all the others, Levinas sometimes writes, and I more than all the others. Further, the fact that these arguments are founded on the thought of a revelation of absolute otherness brings them, and Levinas' ethics, into essential contact with religion. Again, Burggraeve does not hesitate to press this contact toward a theology inspired by Levinas. The way to that new theology appears to aim toward the connection between Athens (philosophy) and Jerusalem (prophetic religion). Burggraeve records that focus perhaps most memorably in the final sentence of this illuminating book: "Levinas is to be seen "working out a great phenomenological foundation and elaboration of a single proposition, namely, that the biblical command 'thou shalt not kill' is, in metaphysics and in ethics, both the first word and the last word on the level of responsibility, and on the level of justice it is the ground of peace and human rights."

David A. Boileau
Loyola University
New Orleans, Louisiana

CHAPTER I
EMMANUEL LEVINAS: THINKER BETWEEN JERUSALEM AND ATHENS
AN INTRODUCTORY PHILOSOPHICAL BIOGRAPHY

Emmanuel Levinas died a few days before he would have been 90 years old, on December 25, 1995, very early Monday morning, in the Paris clinic of Beaujon, where he had been admitted the previous day with serious heart complications.

This introductory philosophical biography wishes to do justice to one of the greats of Western philosophy, as well as of dialogical thinking in particular, by probing the lines of force and movements of intellectual growth in his thinking. It wishes especially to bring into relief the bipolarity of Levinas' personality as a thinker: on one hand, he is in reality 'Jewish,' while on the other hand he is also fully a 'Westerner.' He thus moves constantly between the poles Jerusalem and Athens, or between *prophecy* and *philosophy* (**TI** XII/24). Nonetheless, he is a philosopher in the strict sense of the word, never making use of the Bible or Jewish texts as an argument or proof of a reflexive standpoint, but instead, at most, to illustrate a point. This does not take away the fact that, as is the case with every thinker, Levinas' '*expériences naturelles*,' or 'pre-philosophical experiences' (De Waelhens)—that is to say, his basic Jewish experiences—always enliven his philosophical thinking. But he also remains a philosopher even in his typically Jewish writings, where he is always intent upon translating Jewish insights and texts into 'Greek' (**HN** 156/134)—in other words, to lay bare their metaphysical, anthropological and ethical dimensions, and then to make them reflexively communicable (**DL** 36/19).

THE JERUSALEM POLE

Levinas was born in Kovno (present-day Kaunas), Lithuania, on December 30, 1905—at least according to the Julian calendar then still in use in Czarist Russia and the surrounding regions; according to our Gregorian calendar, this falls on January 12, 1906. As capitol of the province and an important cultural center, Kovno was at that time one of the larger cities in Lithuania, with Estonia and Latvia one of the three Baltic states bordered by White Russia in the east. Levinas belonged to a moderately well-off middle class family which had risen through business and hard work. His father was the book dealer Jehiel Levinas and his mother was Dvòra Gurvitch.

From his earliest youth, he was entrusted to a private tutor in 'modern' Hebrew and, by extension, the Bible. These private lessons, given henceforth in a continuous and intense rhythm, ran parallel with his elementary and middle school years, until 1918. Not even the various migrations and wanderings of his family during the first world war put an end to it. With respect to the Hebrew he studied then, the adjective 'modern' does not signify another language than that of the Bible, but reflects a conception of Hebrew as a modern language, which is to say as a language free from the 'dominion' of religious texts, though without neglecting the study of biblical texts in Hebrew. In the same 'modern' spirit of his milieu, he received no instruction in the Talmud (understood as the historical whole of Rabbinic commentaries on, and interpretations of the Law of Moses), which he would later emphasize as essential for Judaism. Levinas' original Jewish formation must thus in fact be designated as general, and not typically Talmudic.

BACKGROUND IN MITNAGGED-JUDAISM

However, this general Jewish background *was* colored by *mitnagged-*Judaism. Literally, 'mitnagged' means 'opponent.' The object of this opposition was *hasidism*. Hasidism came into existence mid-way through the 18th century as a sort of devotional Judaism among the frequently illiterate rural Jews of the Ukrainian provinces of what was then Poland—Volhynia, Podolia and Galicia. The great impulse came from Israël ben Eliëzer (1700-1760), also known as Baäl Shem

Tov, meaning 'friendly Master of the Name (of God),' and 'possessor of the good name,' or 'entrusted with the people.' He taught that the true religion consisted not necessarily in the study of Jewish texts, but in an immediate, sincere and joyous love of God. The core of this living religiosity is *enthusiasm* ('hitlahawoet'), literally 'being in God' ('en-theos-eimi'), as Buber has pointed out in *Die Erzählungen der Chassidim* (1965). The enthusiastic were called 'tsaddikim.' The just were more correctly referred to as 'the-seemingly-just' or 'those-who-are-found-righteous,' whereas the enthusiastic were called the 'hasidim,' the pious, those who place their trust in the covenant, forming the hasidic community led by the tsaddikim. This enthusiasm expressed itself concretely in direct participation in, and heartfelt experience of God's omnipresence, both in fervent prayer and in daily life, with all of its tasks and duties.

Hasidism met with heavy resistance, especially among the Jews of Lithuania and White Russia. In those places, a sober and intellectual Judaism predominated—one sustained in the discipline of studying the Talmud. Resistance to hasidism was initiated by Elijah ben Solomon (1720-1797), also called the Gaon of Vilna (Vilnius, still the capitol of Lithuania), and was carried on further by the 'mitnaggedim,' or opponents. According to Levinas, Elijah ben Solomon was one of the last truly great geniuses of the Talmud. He was also the founder of the Yeshiva, or 'academy of higher study of the Talmud,' where the Talmud was no longer studied privately but in a group and under the direction of a learned teacher. In his Jewish writings, Levinas points several times to Rabbi Chaïm Voloziner (1789-1821), the favorite student of the Gaon of Vilna. He even dedicates a detailed and penetrating study to him, which at the same time also throws considerable light on his own thinking: "A l'image de Dieu, d'après Rabbi Haïm Voloziner" (1977) (**ID**) (**AV** 182-200/151-167). In a much later study, "Judaïsme et kénose" (1985) (**JK**), he explicitly retraces his thinking (**HN** 138-151/114-132). Levinas indicates how in eastern Europe, Lithuania was the land—and Vilnius in particular the city—where Judaism reached its spiritual peak. The level of Talmud-study was extremely elevated and there ruled a 'Jewish life' that was based on that study and even experienced *as* study. The land

of Levinas' birth was clearly dominated by an intellectual Judaism
(**EFP** 64).

Levinas, then, was clearly influenced by mitnagged Judaism, not so
much by a specific ideas as by a general underlying trend in spirituality. Though the resistance of the mitnaggedim to the hasidim died
down after some time, still the two ways of being Jewish never flowed
historically into one another. This shows up not only in the use of two
different prayer books in their respective liturgies, but especially in the
greater emphasis in hasidism on emotionality, inwardness, subjectivity and the 'experience of God,' in contrast with the accent on the
rationality of the outwardly objective, 'strict application' of Talmud-
study in mitnagged Judaism. Without the sharp edges of this contrast,
the difference was still real enough when Levinas was ushered into
Jewish life. It is above all by this difference of accent in climate and
tone that Levinas was marked as a Jew. And it is against this mitnagged
background that we can understand his almost instinctive—and,
according to some, even exaggerated and obsessional—reservations
about mystical enthusiasm, as well as any so-called specifically religious 'awakening' [*réveil*], with its constant recurrence of nostalgia for
a heartfelt and 'pathetic' religious experience of intense 'internaliza-
tion' and 'spirit.' His first collection of essays on Judaism, *Difficile
Liberté* (**DL**), appearing first in 1963 and then again, reworked and
expanded, in 1976, is a pregnant illustration of the basic mitnagged
rationality from which Levinas interprets Judaism and calls for an
intellectual and philosophical approach to the 'Jewish texts,' which
according to him 'give to think'—that is, represent a specific form of
thinking by which they resist the tests of an insistent and 'strict,'
critical reflection.

In fact, Levinas' mitnagged rationality influences not only his interaction with Jewish texts and traditions, but also equally his philosophical thinking. His intellectual Judaism meets with the western
preference for thinking such as is manifest in Greek thought and
renewed in the Enlightenment. Both Jewish and western intellectualism reinforce one another in his thinking, arriving at what he himself refers to as 'his trust in the intellectualism of reason.' (**TI** XVII)

INTELLECTUAL APPROACH TO JEWISH TEXTS

It is not until 1947 that Levinas begins to apply himself rigorously to the Talmud. This he did under the direction of Chouchani, 'illustrious and inexorable master of exegesis and the Talmud' (**DL** 373/ 291), whom according to Levinas represented the summum of what mitnagged Judaism had to offer.[1] Chouchani's intellectually inventive conception of the Talmud brought Levinas to register his basic Hebrew experiences in the language of western philosophy. The results of this work can be met with in his Talmud lessons, which he delivered almost yearly at gatherings of French-speaking Jewish intellectuals in Paris, and which were collected in *Quatre lectures talmudiques* (1968) (**QLT**), *Du sacré au saint. Cinq nouvelles lectures talmudiques* (1977) (**SaS**), *L'au-delà du verset. Lectures et discours talmudiques* (1982) (**AV**), *A l'heure des nations* (1988) (**HN**) and *Nouvelles lectures talmudiques* (1996) (**NLT**). Via the Talmud, understood as the work of *wise men* and not of priests, prophets or theologians, he also considers the Bible not primarily as the sum of revealed truths which—interpreted by a sanctioned power—must be accepted, but as a thinking with at least as much authority in philosophy as do the verses of the Presocratics, Homer, Trakl or Hölderlin.... Such a conception is based on the characteristically Talmudic conviction that Scripture, as the expression of a culture which is human and not only religious, can contain a powerful rationality and thus both can and may be accessible to an exacting form of thought, or rather is itself already an original, perhaps 'idiosyncratic' form of thinking, and for that very reason is captivating and intriguing (**DL** 352/274).

In 1946, Levinas became director of Paris' *Ecole Normale Israélite Orientale*, which educated French teachers for the Jewish elementary schools in the region of the Mediterranean Sea (including, among others, Tunisia and Morocco). In this function, which he retained until beginning his university career in 1961 (**EFP** 87), he strongly encouraged a free and consistent intellectual commitment to the study of the written sources of the Jewish traditions. In connection with his efforts to expand the *Ecole Normale Israélite Orientale* from 'Ecole de maîtres' ['school of teachers'] to 'Ecole de cadres' ['school of intellectuals'], Levinas wanted to free Judaism from its culturally privatized and 'clericalized' ghetto. During the postwar period of the 1950s and 1960s, his zeal for an 'intellectual Jewish laity' did not cease. Judaism can survive only if it is recognized and handed down through the laity (**DL** 322/250-51). This intellectual lay Judaism is possible only if Jewish texts, which in the traditionalist orthodoxy are reserved for the ministers of the cultus, are freed from these—often dogmatizing or apologetic—monopolies and studied anew. For the Jewish texts to 'nourish spirits, they must once again nourish brains' (**DL** 343/267). They must become the object of thinking, not of an affected historical-archaeological erudition but of a rigorous thinking which so interrogates and discusses them with a critical 're-'thinking that it surrenders to them its 'teachings,' namely its life-giving insights on humanity, the world, society and God. This 'Jewish thinking' is, according to Levinas himself, the principle condition for the survival of Judaism (**DL** 330-331/258). Only such a transhistorical concep-tion of Jewish texts makes possible an indispensable 'Jewish intellec-tual elite' which by its reflexive appropriation of essentially Hebrew texts could be the true 'teachers' of Judaism. In 1959, Levinas also dreamed of a network of centers of Jewish education in Paris, including his *Ecole Normale* and especially the *Centre Universitaire d'Etudes Juives*, in order to bring the ever-growing number of young, university-schooled intellectuals together into a large reflection group, or better into a movement. It was not without humor that he designated this movement the 'Ecole de Paris,' since those interested came mainly not from France but Oran and Obernaï, Moscow, Kiev, Tunis and elsewhere (**QLT** 23/9). This involvement in the formation of a specifically Jewish intelligentsia also led him now and then to address Jewish texts, in particular the Talmud, as a philosopher—the results of which can be seen in the aforementioned 'Talmudic lessons and discourses.'

EXPERIENCE OF RACIST PERSECUTION

Another important aspect of Levinas' Jewish background is what we can call his experience of racist persecution. As a child he had heard much tell of the 'pogroms,' or popular outbursts of rage against the Jews in Czarist Russia between 1881 and 1917. At the age of eleven, he himself went through the Bolshevik October Revolution (1917) in Ukraine, when his family fled the violence of the war in several steps—which consequently meant that, properly speaking, he had only a very short childhood (**EFP** 63). During this period, he also became closely acquainted with the bitter violence of the persecution of the Jews. The initially pro-Jewish position of Lenin and the Bolsheviks, among whom there were many Jews, explains why the Jews were made to suffer so greatly by the counter-revolutionaries who emerged especially in White Russia and Ukraine against the Bolshevik Red Army, and who were supported by the western Allies. Wherever the so-called White Army entered, there followed a wave of terror and violence against the local Jews. In connection with these outbursts, Levinas later testified in a letter (1975) that the Russian revolution 'signified [for him] the beginning of all further developments.'[2]

The wound of this racist persecution was thus inscribed on Levinas indelibly by the extermination of the Jews perpetrated by Hitler and the SS both before and during the second world war. In the autobiographical piece "Signature," he writes: 'This biography is dominated by a presentiment of the Nazi terror and its memory thereafter' (**DL** 374/291). Concerning the period 1933-1939, when that presentiment became ever clearer, he writes: 'Imagine the atmosphere of this period 1933-1939, as if the end of the world approached! How the war approached and how the swastika, cheered by the masses, spread!' (**DL** 220-221/168) From out of this apocalyptic threat of the unraveling of history itself, Levinas wrote already in 1935: 'Hitlerism is the greatest test, the most incomparable test, that Judaism has ever had to endure. The moral and physical suffering that the German Jews were supposed to expect from Hitlerism and had also already received from it, surpassed in excessive manner the persistence (and toughness) for which they are famous from of old.' Among them—not only from Germany but, as a result of the war, the whole of Europe—whether it was by chance, a lapse on the part of the Gestapo, or the oblivion of destiny, those numbering among the survivors of the Nazi persecution were in the literal sense of the word 'marked.' There was preserved on their flesh a biting wound, as if they had seen the Forbidden and Unspeakable from too close, and forever afterwards had to bear the shame of having survived it (**DL** 337/263).

The whole of Levinas' thinking can be interpreted as an immense effort to bring to light the roots of violence and racism, and as an attempt to overcome this in principle by *thinking otherwise*. This 'thinking otherwise' is developed from the beginning as a thinking about the 'other,' since according to Levinas the other is precisely that which is denied in racism. For him, evil lies in 'being' in so far as the being—expressed eminently in his or her effort to be—absorbs the other into itself. It is this same evil, the evil of the 'reduction of the other to the same,' that Levinas discovers in antisemitism, as the radical intensification of racism. In antisemitism, hate is directed at the Jew as intolerable other. In racism, the enemy is the other as such. In other words, the other is the enemy not on the ground of his or personality, various characteristics, one or another activity considered bothersome or morally objectionable, but simply by reason of his or her very otherness. In antisemitism, it is the other who is always guilty, and the ego itself—as embodiment of the 'same' which not only draws everything to itself but also poses as their principle of meaning and value. Well now, according to Levinas it is precisely this evil, the fundamental evil of antisemitism and all racism, that must be combatted. Hence does he, speaking form out of his experience of racist persecution, define ethics by attention and respect for the other *as* other, by doing justice to the other, by unconditional responsibility for the other in his or her otherness, which he also calls 'goodness.' At first sight, this goodness seems a simple, or even banal idea, but for Levinas it loses this simplicity in light of the evil that it is to overcome. His fundamental idea of care for the other—an other who is always 'stranger'—presupposes or, stronger still, reaches its full power in light of the racist denial and eradication of the other. Such an idea of goodness is the complete contrary of a cheap and naive thought, good only for pious souls or idealistic adolescents not yet experienced in life's realities. Goodness as turn toward the other is not a self-evident, 'natural' idea emerging spontaneously in our day-to-day lives. On the contrary, it sets forth an 'inverted order,' an 'Umwertung aller Werte,' going radically against the current of our 'ordinary' existence—against, that is, existence itself. Only by understanding this goodness as the contrary of antisemitism and racism can its true, revolutionary and counter-intuitive character emerge. To employ one useful image—an image which comes from Levinas himself—goodness goes so far that it keeps the cold in and for itself while we by nature rather appreciate the warmth. The true meaning and real value of goodness, understood as unconditional involvement with the other, consists precisely in overcoming the evil threatening the other with reduction and destruction by establishing another relation with him or her—one resting on attentive respect which permits or pursues justice for him or her. In this sense, the Levinasian idea of responsibility for the other can never be thought or explained without also pointing to its counterpart, its negative inverse which it resists in particular, namely the evil of hate, not of the human in general, but of the other person, of the alterity of the other person. On the basis of his experience of persecution, the thinking of Levinas has become an antiracist thinking *par excellence*!

Finally, Levinas' emigration to France in 1923 also had something to do with antisemitism. The regulations promulgated by the communists beginning in 1919-1920 against Zionism and prohibiting (Jewish) religious instruction, were the reason that Levinas, like so many other Russian Jews, left at age 18—with a stop in Germany— for France, where for the Jewish communities of eastern Europe the prophecies became reality. Levinas settled in Strasbourg where, after a year spent studying French and Latin, he began university studies in philosophy. It was at that time that he also established a friendship with Maurice Blanchot, who came to Strasbourg two or three years after him and with whom he spent much of the remainder of his study time. Later, it was Blanchot who provided refuge for Levinas' wife during the wartime occupation of France, while Levinas himself was a prisoner of the Germans. Levinas revered in Blanchot the image 'of a keen intelligence and an aristocratic thinking' (**EFP** 71), though as a monarchist Blanchot subscribed to very different political ideas than did Levinas himself. Through their strong friendship, they had during their Strasbourg period frequent access to one another's thinking, so that their developed a mutual influence later becoming evident in, among other things, the fact that each points in his work to that of the other and finds related ideas there. Levinas consecrated a number of studies exclusively to Blanchot, of which four have been collected in *Sur Maurice Blanchot* (1975) (**MB**).

Levinas' teachers in Strasbourg included Maurice Pradines, professor of general philosophy, Charles Blondel, who taught a sharply anti-Freudian psychology, the sociologist Maurice Halbwachs, and Henri Carteron, who taught ancient philosophy and, upon his death, was succeeded by Martial Guéroult—all of whom were still young during the time of the 'Dreyfus affair.' Through their influence, Levinas—as newcomer—was struck by 'the blinding vision of a people that stands equal humanity, and of a nation to which one can attach oneself with heart and soul as strongly as if from there by origin' (**DL** 373/291). By this, he refers to the humanist ideals of the French revolution, 'liberty, equality and fraternity,' which stand above every narrow principle of nationality, making human rights the foundation of humane society (**HS** 175). He thus also calls France 'le pays des Droits de l'homme' ['the nation of human rights'] (**DL** 332/259).

THE ATHENS POLE

The western influence on Levinas does not begin in Strasbourg, but dates from all the way back in his early youth. On his own account, the lion's share of his intellectual training was not typically Jewish but western. Notwithstanding the fact that early 20th century Lithuania Judaism was still permeated by the intellectual mitnagged Judaism, or that the generations (including the parents of the young Levinas) continued to familiarize their children with Hebrew, they saw greater advantages and a brighter future in the Russian language and culture. Accordingly, Russian literature played a particularly important role in Levinas' general formation: it held an importance and prestige which always stayed with Levinas, despite his later penetrating western European formation.

FROM RUSSIAN LITERATURE TO PHENOMENOLOGY

Because his parents, as 'assimilated' Jews, did not live in the so-called Jewish neighborhood of *Kovno*, and because they also spoke Russian at home, Levinas immediately became conversant with the classic Russian authors, such as Pushkin, Lermontov, Gogol, Turgenev, Tolstoi, and above all Dostoyevsky, to whom he would later refer regularly. During this same period, he also came into contact with the great western European writers, notably Shakespeare, whom he also cited frequently in his later work and whose *Hamlet*, *Macbeth*, and *King Lear* he especially admired. If one also thinks of certain traumatic experiences, such as a separation, a display of violence, or an abrupt awareness of the monotony of time, leaving one in search of words only to find none, it is according to Levinas precisely through the reading of books that these original shock experiences and all their blind and hesitant groping lead to questions and problems. Books give rise to thought. They do not merely present us with words, but make it possible to take part in 'the true life that is absent' from us without being either utopic or impossible. As opposed to a mistrust of 'book-learning,' which considers each book as no more than a source of information, a 'tool for study' or a 'handbook,' Levinas has always had a penetrating sensitivity to the 'ontological' bearing of the book as the very modality of our human existence. To that end, it is certainly not necessary that these books be of a philosophical strain. To the contrary, they can just as well—or even preferably—be novels, poetry, theater pieces and such. In this respect, the Russian classics and Shakespeare were for Levinas a good preparation for Plato and Kant and the philosophical problem of the 'meaning of the human,' or of the 'meaning of life'—questions which the characters in the Russian novels raise continually (**EI** 15-16/22). To read is to raise oneself up to, to listen to and obey exteriority, the essentially new which does not rise up from within ourselves but breaks in upon us as a 'revelation' from the foreign, touching us such that we—while remaining ourselves—become radically 'other.'

When Levinas arrived in Strasbourg in 1923, he immediately began his higher studies, which he crowned in 1927, with a 'Licenses ès Lettres.' As preparation for his doctorate in philosophy, he began in that same year—1923—to study phenomenology, under Jean Héring (1890-1966), who became 'maître des conférences' at the Protestant faculty of the University of Strasbourg in 1926 and shortly thereafter was named ordinary professor at the same faculty (where he would remain until October of 1954, when he would step down due to poor health). Levinas turned to Héring because he was the most suitable person in Strasbourg to introduce him to phenomenology. In 1925, Héring published his own doctorate in philosophy, with the title

'Phénoménologie et philosophie religieuse.' This was the first study to appear in France which offered an extensive treatment of the growing phenomenological movement (and thus not on Husserl alone), which he had come to know during a study visit to Göttingen, where he made personal contact with Edmund Husserl and the so-called 'Göttingen circle' that he had gathered around himself. This group included Moritz Geiger, Theodor Conrad, Dietrich Von Hildebrand, Hedwig Conrad-Martius, Alexander Koyré, Roman Ingarden, Fritz Kaufmann, and Edith Stein. Héring's introduction to phenomenology caught hold of Levinas so much that he himself decided to deepen his knowledge of this new philosophical movement under the direction of the great master, Husserl. He therefore departed in 1928 for the German city Freiburg in Bresgau, where Husserl had been teaching since 1916. Levinas remained in Freiburg for two semesters: the summer semester of 1928 (March-July) and the winter semester of 1928-1929 (October-February) (**PA** 122-123). During the summer semester, he took part in the final series of seminars of Husserl's career and gave a presentation at the very last meeting at the end of July. During that semester, he also attended the occasional and highly sought conferences held by Husserl in place of the required instruction from which he gradually withdrew by the end of the winter semester in order to devote himself to the publication of his many manuscripts. Levinas not only studied under Husserl, but also made personal contact with him and even visited him at home. This testifies to the fact that Levinas was invited to give Husserl's wife Malvina some private lessons in French (in order to offer Levinas the student some financial support without coming as simple 'charity'). This occurred in preparation for an imminent journey to Paris, where Husserl was invited to speak about phenomenology. It was out these lectures that the soon to be famous *Cartesianische Meditationen* were to grow, and which were translated from the German into French by Gabrielle Pfeiffer, who attended to the first part, and Levinas, who undertook the remainder—namely, the fourth and fifth lectures. This translation appeared as *Méditations cartésiennes. Introduction à la phénoménologie par Edmund Husserl* (1931) (**MC**).

According to Levinas, the atmosphere in Freiburg was completely dominated by Husserl's phenomenology: though it is also the city of medicine, chemistry and so many other sciences, Freiburg is foremost 'the city of phenomenology' (cf. his 1931 article, "Fribourg, Husserl et la phénoménologie'; **FHP**). The longstanding presence of Husserl and his gradually more famous phenomenology attracted a great many students from the whole of Germany and beyond its borders. There ruled a spirit of intense purpose and 'devotion' to phenomenology. 'Working' was the word of order in the 'city of Husserl.' The young phenomenologists, proud of being students of the great master, considered themselves at work for philosophical discoveries as occur in the positive sciences. They hoped—and were indeed convinced— that they would realize Husserl's dream of a 'rigorously scientific philosophy' through the tireless efforts of each succeeding generation of 'philosophical workers.' This 'ivresse de travail' ['intoxication with work'] went together with an almost euphoric joy and a refreshing enthusiasm. For them, Husserl's phenomenology was more than a new theory. It was an ideal to live by, a new phase in history, almost a new religion. They believed in a new springtime, a new renaissance, a re-awakening of the 'spirit' which would be in position to answer all questions.

The first result of Levinas' intensive study is an expanded 'review'— 36 pages long—which he published in 1929, on Husserl's *Ideen zu einer reinen Phänomenologie und phänomenologische Philosophie. Erstes Buch: Allgemeine Einführung in die reine Phänomenologie* (**SIH**), which had appeared in 1913, as the first issue of a series published by Husserl himself, the *Jahrbuch für Philosophie und phänomenologische Forschung*. Levinas' summary overview of this work was at the same time his first philosophical publication. In April of 1930, he received his doctorate in philosophy in Strasbourg, with a thesis on Husserlian phenomenology: *La théorie de l'intuition dans la phénoménologie de Husserl* (**TIPH**). This dissertation was crowned by the *Académie des Sciences Morales et Politiques* of the *Institut de France*, so that it appeared in book form already in 1931. As one of the first basic monographic and systematic works on Husserl, it played an important role in the introduction of Husserlian phenomenology to the French-speaking world. It is known, for instance, that Sartre came into contact with Husserl via Levinas' dissertation (**PA** 124-125). And indeed, it remains an interesting means to becoming acquainted with

Husserlian phenomenology. After his dissertation, Levinas wrote a number of other penetrating studies on Husserl, above all around 1959, on the occasion of the centennial of Husserl's birth: 'Réflexions sur la 'technique' phénoménologique' (**RTP**), 'La ruine de la représentation' (**RR**), 'Intentionalité et métaphysique' (**IM**), and then, in 1965, 'Intentionalité et sensation' (**IS**). All of these contributions were taken up in the second, expanded edition of Levinas' *En découvrant l'existence avec Husserl et Heidegger* (1967) (**DEHH**).

For his own thinking, Levinas found in Husserlian phenomenology above all a *method*, which directed him to a radical reflection reaching beyond or beneath what appears at first glance, to what has been forgotten but which nonetheless supports the appearing—for example, beyond (Heideggerian) Being to the *responsibility to and for the other*. This perspective on Husserl is evident, among other places, in the noteworthy study, 'De la conscience à la veille. A partir de Husserl' (1974) (**CV**), in which Levinas begins from the Husserlian method and categories, but radicalizes the Husserlian deepening of consciousness into an analysis of its pre-conscious 'underground,' until arriving at his own (Levinas') vision of consciousness as 'vigilance toward-the-other despite oneself.' This vigilance as-attachment-to-the-other rests not with an active and alert attention, but is awakened in the subject by the 'always already passed' other, and in such a manner that the subject is also 'established,' or grounded.

During his stay in Freiburg, Levinas also came into contact with Heidegger, who succeeded Husserl in 1929, but had been teaching there already since 1928. It is especially the insightful phenomenological analyses of *Sein und Zeit* (1927) that Levinas has since mentioned. His acquaintance with Heidegger in fact took place in the context of an ongoing *confrontation* between Husserl and Heidegger, both of whom were teaching at that time. This confrontation extended to their students, who leaned in favor of Heidegger (about whom Levinas would later have feelings much more ambivalent than at that early date).

That Husserl and Heidegger must not be considered as two completely distinct sources for Levinas' thinking can be seen in his publication of a collection of essays on both thinkers in a single work: *En découvrant l'existence avec Husserl et Heidegger* (first edition, 1949).

This (already mentioned) work portrays Levinas' early meeting with phenomenology and its *existential* interpretation, and at the same time testifies to the expectations awakened by this encounter.

However, Levinas quickly distanced himself from Heidegger, and not only personally, when in 1933 Heidegger briefly lent his support to the Nazi regime, accepting the rectorship at Freiburg and wearing the brown shirt and swastika—but also on the field of thought. In his later, original works, Levinas repeatedly confronts Heidegger, and above all his vision of Being and ontology. This has led to frequent references to his own work as pronouncedly *anti-Heideggerian*, although he himself certainly did not stake such a strong claim.

OTHERWISE THAN HEIDEGGER: THE WAY TO THE OTHER

From 1930 to 1932, Levinas carried on philosophical studies at the Sorbonne, in Paris. One of his teachers was the Jew, Léon Brunschvicq, whose *rational* neo-idealism fit well with Levinas' mitnagged background. In Paris, Levinas also came into contact with Jean Wahl, and learned to prize both his intellectual, anti-intellectualist subtlety and his warm friendship. Jean Wahl was also Levinas' promoter when he delivered *Totalité et Infini* (**TI**) in 1961, in order to receive the grade of doctorat d'état.

During the 1930s, Levinas also met with the avant-garde philosophers who gathered on Saturday evenings at the home of Gabriel Marcel. Whenever Levinas refers in his work to Marcel, he always connects it with the I-Thou thinking of Martin Buber, who also exercised a deep influence on him, though not without receiving a degree of criticism. Levinas considered himself as someone who tried especially to bring out the metaphysical and ethical dimensions of the *interhuman*, in the line of Marcel and Buber, but at the same time going further, surpassing them.

Another great Jewish thinker who has deeply influenced Levinas is Franz Rosenzweig (1886-1929), with his resistance to the Hegelian idea of totality (**TI** XVI/28), return to Judaism after the 'assimilation movement,' and, in particular, (extremely difficult) master work, *Stern der Erlösung* (1921). Levinas came upon and studied Rosenzweig's work in 1935 (**EFP** 121). He also devoted explicit attention to it in two essays, 'Entre deux mondes. (Biographie spirituelle de Franz Rosenzweig)' (1963) (**EDM**) (**DL** 235-260/181-201), and 'Franz Rosenzweig: une pensée juive moderne' (1965) (**FR**) (**HS** 71-96), as well as in the detailed 'Préface' (**P**) to Stéphane Mosès' book, *Système et Révélation. La philosophie de Franz Rosenzweig* (1982).

In 1963, Levinas was named docent in philosophy at the Faculty of Letters in Poitiers. In 1967, he became professor at Paris-Nanterre, where he taught the history of philosophy and commented on the texts of such great thinkers as Kant, Hegel, Husserl and Heidegger. In 1973, he was promoted to full professor at the Sorbonne, in Paris, where he taught until becoming emeritus in 1976. His final courses, 'La mort et le temps' and 'Dieu et l'onto-théo-logie,' given at the Sorbonne in 1975-1976, were published much later, through the efforts of one of his eminent students, Jacques Rolland. They appear together under the single title, *Dieu, la mort et le temps* (1991, 1993) (**DMT**).

It is possible to distinguish a number of periods in Levinas' thinking. One thus begins with a period of 'apprenticeship,' situated between 1923 and 1935, in which he grounded himself in both phenomenology and, at the same time, dialogical—or Jewish—thinking. His second period, during which his own, original thinking begins to emerge, can be situated beginning in 1935, the year in which appeared his first penetrating, independent study, 'De l'Evasion' (much later, in 1982, this article was published in book form, introduced and annotated by the aforementioned Jacques Rolland) (**EVA**). Levinas himself has described the evolution of his thinking thereafter in terms of the following three discoveries: (1) *being without beings* (what he calls the 'il y a' ['there is']); (2) the movement from *anonymous being* to the *being* [or entity], and the *separated ego* in particular; and finally (3) the way leading from the separated being to the *face of the other*, with its ethical implication of *responsibility-to-and-for-the-other* as well as the metaphysical implication of *desire for the wholly other*, or for the Infinite, the context in which a 'being-toward-God' uncontaminated by being can acquire its true meaning.

The first two points of this evolution emerge primarily in *De l'existence à l'existant* (**EE**) and *Le temps et l'autre* (**TA**), both of which appeared in 1947. These works supply only the impetus for a third step, which virtually 'exploded' in Levinas' first major work, *Totalité et Infini* (**TI**), fourteen years later. The studies appearing after this book further work out its metaphysical, anthropological and ethical perspective. This can be seen in the aforementioned second, expanded edition of *En découvrant l'existence avec Husserl et Heidegger* (**DEHH**). This new edition includes 'La philosophie et l'idée de l'Infini' (**PIF**), an article from 1957 which explicitly announces the central themes of *Totalité et Infini*, as well as several studies following immediately from that first major work. In a number of subsequent studies, such as 'La trace de l'autre' (1963) (**TRA**) and especially 'Enigme et phénomène' (1965) (**EP**), there begins to emerge the outline of Levinas' second and perhaps most mature major work, *Autrement qu'être ou au-delà de l'essence* (**AE**), which was published in 1974. As a sort of interim balance, there appeared in 1972 the collection, *Humanisme de l'autre homme* (**HAH**). After the appearance of *Autrement qu'être*, which focuses above all on redefining the subject as 'responsibility-to-and-for-the-other,' and isolating its metaphysical 'trace' in a 'thinking-to-God,' a number of further studies are then centered on working out in a strictly philosophical way its 'theological' implications. This were collected and published under the title *De Dieu qui vient à l'idée* (**DVI**), in 1982. In that same year, Levinas also published *Ethique et Infini* (**EI**), a series of radio broadcasts with Philippe Nemo, in which a number of the insights fundamental for his entire oeuvre are sketched in a concise and accessible manner, and linked together. This work serves well as an introduction to his thought which does justice to the ideas appearing before, in and after *Totalité et Infini*. Since then, still more of Levinas' studies have appeared in collections, including—but not exclusively—a number of early studies which had not yet been made available in book form. Among these are *Hors sujet* (1987) (**HS**), *Entre nous. Essais sur le penser-à-l'autre* (1991) (**EN**), *Emmanuel Levinas* (1991) (**EL**), *Liberté et commandement* (1994) (**LC**), *Les imprévus de l'histoire* (1994) (**IH**) and *Altérité et transcendance* (1995) (**AT**).

The basic constant in all of Levinas' writings remains from beginning to end his search for the idea of a Good beyond being. He finds this idea in us as the 'an-archic' fundamental condition in which we find ourselves as subjects, and which we also discover through the ethical appeal to an unconditional responsibility that the face of the other awakens in us by its appearance as 'the poor, the widow and the orphan': 'éveil du moi par autrui' ['awakening of the I by the other']. From this ethics of heteronomy which also forms this basis for a radical redefinition of human rights, there runs a metaphysical trace 'to-God' ('à-Dieu') as a desire for the wholly Other, or the Infinite. This desire arises not out of simple wish or lack in the I, but is awakened in the I by the epiphany of the face, and deepened into one which is insatiable. And it is precisely in this desire which does not aim at emancipation because it was not born out of hunger that the divine Infinite can reveal itself as the inspiring 'spirit' of the Good.

CONCLUSION

The effort of composing this introductory philosophical biography leaves behind some ambivalent feelings. It has unwillingly borrowed too much from photography or imagery. And yet, 'the other is invisible,' as Levinas himself has radically expressed it, thus opposing himself to the frequent misunderstanding in the 'face' of the other is confused with his or her 'countenance,' which is to say with his or her appearance and describability, physiognomy, personality or character, familial and social status, intellectual and religious origin and background, and so forth. What Levinas refers to as the 'face' is precisely that which exceeds the 'countenance.' This implies that every attempt to make him or her visible through one or another—even intellectual—'account of life' already involves a form of misunderstanding and injustice which begs for the 'c'est-à-dire' of the correction. The present introductory philosophical biography must therefore be read as a pressing invitation to study Levinas' texts themselves, for the spoken word, of which the written word is an embodiment addressed to-the-reader—reveals the other.

This textual study is then also pre-eminently an ethical event in which we are called by what comes 'from elsewhere' and both places us in question and asks for our hospitality. Yet, here too the other remains invisible, in the sense that the other never gives itself to a text without at the same time also withdrawing from it. This latter is the case in that, regardless of how it is consecrated, any study—literally, any application to a text—can not but be uttered according to individual manners of understanding and interpretation. In his texts, Levinas remains the 'other' who can never be reduced to one or another conception of him, which would be a form of violence. His transcendence thus also brings out his vulnerability, by which his readers, interpreters and commentators are, as it were, both 'charmed' and 'incited' to come to terms with his otherness. Here, it is also possible to see the ethical significance of reading Levinas' writing, specifically where it articulates the prohibition 'Thou shall not kill.' What *is* of course possible, and even obvious—reducing the other to his or her countenance or appearance (in the text)—*must* not be done. Positively stated, this prohibition expresses the appeal to do justice to the other (that is, to Levinas, as he speaks to us through his texts). And this justice makes possible the truth. The answer to the appeal of the other going out from his texts, puts us on the trail of the truth which, thanks precisely to the ethical relation of 'gratitude' becomes true knowledge of Levinas spoken and still speaking to us through his texts, without itself becoming the final and definitive word. We hope that the reading of this book will appeal to a reflective study of Levinas' writings, even if they do not reveal their wisdom all at once.

---

[1] Levinas' encounter and relationship with Chouchani is discussed at length in S. Malka, *Monsieur Chouchani. L'énigme d'un maître du XXᵉ siècle*, Paris, Ed. J.-C. Lattès, 1994, pp. 111-114.

[2] "Antwoord van Emmanuel Levinas" (in French) to R. Burggraeve, "Questions posées à Monsieur Emmanuel Levinas, le 10 juillet 1975," published in R. Burggraeve en L. Anckaert (red.), *De Vele Gezichten van het Kwaad. Meedenken in Het Spoor van Emmanuel Levinas*, Acco, Leuven / Amersfoort, 1996, pp. 184-188.

CHAPTER 2
JUSTICE, PEACE AND HUMAN RIGHTS CENTERED ON THE EGO

As Levinas' thinking progresses, peace and human rights become increasingly important themes. In the writings of the last two decades of his life they even become virtual synonyms for his central concept of responsibility. In order to achieve good insight into his ethical and political conception of peace and human rights, we will approach it from a study of the *Grundanliegen* of his thinking on the "responsibility prior to freedom." But in order to truly grasp the originality and radicality of his vision, it is first helpful to review the sketch which he has provided of mainstream "western philosophy," which approaches peace and human rights according to a responsibility defined in terms of individual freedom and well-managed private interest. This path through Levinas' conception of western philosophy clarifies how he overcomes what he considers an "egocentric" definition of responsibility precisely by returning to the proper essence of peace and human rights that has, from his perspective, been covered over. Accordingly, and using the language of Husserl, we can consider Levinas' thinking on responsibility, peace, and human rights as a return *zu den Sachen selbst*—a return to real but forgotten conditions of experience and existence. Levinas' thinking, in other words, consists in penetrating to the deeper strata of the human subject— beneath freedom and self-interest—until it becomes clear how a person is structured, or "created," as an ethical "being to-and-for-the-other person." Here, at this level, one is found to be in peaceful unity with the other person and with all other others, both near and far, both present and future. This unity is not necessarily a matter of either physical reality or natural law, but a fundamental ethical call which expresses the rights of the other person. According to Levinas, a peaceful commitment to the rights of the other person comprises our "ethical nature" or basic condition.

RESPONSIBILITY IN THE FIRST PERSON

(BEGINNING FROM THE SELF)

In our culture, there seems to be a firm and indisputable conviction that we can not talk about responsibility unless there is first freedom. In other words, autonomy is seen as the absolute condition for the possibility of responsibility, and as the guarantee for one's own project of existence. We can also refer to this as *responsibility in the first person*, since it begins from the ego and aims at that ego's development. According to Levinas, this sort of responsibility must be taken very seriously, because it is indeed the realization of our human identity and autonomy. For that matter, it is this freedom as responsibility which the classic vision of human rights has always accorded the greatest respect and protection. This requires us to begin by asking how Levinas understands and explains this responsibility in the first person.

THE EGO AS "CONATUS ESSENDI"

Beginning in his second major work, *Autrement qu'être ou au-delà de l'essence* (1974), Levinas describes the ego in synthetic fashion, as "conatus essendi" and "effort of being" (*effort de d'être*) (**AE** 163/ 127). In doing so, he points explicitly to the sixth proposition of the third part of Spinoza's *Ethics*: "Every being does everything it can to persist in its existence" (**NP** 104). This is Spinoza's definition of "being," as that which has no other essence than wanting to be, and that must be understood within the essence of God Himself, the one and all-encompassing Substance of eternal, necessary and perfect Being, of which all beings are modes or ways of being (**VA** 101).

In the course of this characterization of the ego as effort to be, Levinas also refers to Heidegger's description of human Dasein as the being for whom its being is a concern (**CCH** 82). In *Sein und Zeit*, it is said that a person has "to-be," and this having "to-be" is so strong and unavoidable that it becomes Dasein's vocation and singularity.

Heidegger underlines the fact that this singularity is received within the relation to oneself by referring to Dasein's "mineness" (*Jemeinigkeit*) (**AEG** 30).

As a "being," Levinas thus says, the ego is strongly attached to its being, and tries forcefully to establish it (**AS** 63-64). The being of the ego is self-interested: its "esse" is "interesse." It is this that leads him to describe the ego as innately egoistic and tended toward narcissism (**AE** 4/4). This egocentrism, however, is not properly approached solely in negative terms, as if it connotes only base fault or perversion, but must also be understood positively, as the "natural" and perfectly healthy attachment of the ego to itself. Levinas does not hesitate to speak of the ontological necessity of the ego's self-interested dynamic of being: "This self-love is an egoism that founds the being and that constitutes the first ontological experience" (**EFP** 122). Despite the negative connotations which everyday language assigns to the word "egocentrism," we therefore would better speak of the natural egocentrism of the ego.

According to Levinas, the *conatus essendi* of the human ego is at the same time an incarnation of the whole of reality, understood as "Essence": "the meaning of the ego must be referred to Essence, to the task or the vocation to be, that is to say to the carrying out of the activity expressed in the verb of verbs, namely the verb 'to be'" (**DVI** 78). This makes it immediately clear that Levinas' use of the term "Essence" is certainly not to be understood in the sense of "nature," *eidos* or *quidditas*, but in line with what Plato indicated with the expression *nomen actionis*, or active noun. In other words, "Essence" refers to the event of being, whereby we are to understand "being" in its verbal sense, as dynamic process and *actus essendi* (**AE** IX/XLI). For Levinas, "being" is much more than the pure fact of existence; it is the self-contained and self-propelling act of being. This permits him to link it with, for instance, Heidegger's qualititative-dynamic use of the term *Wesen* (or *wesen* as verb) (**CCH** 60). Understood in this way, it is possible to speak of a 'now' or 'present' in this Essence, because it is marked by fundamental self-interest: "its adventure consists in establishing itself in its essence and developing itself in its immanence" (**AE** 19/16). As the energy of being, it runs through and supports all beings, thus constituting a "unity."

From here, Levinas can further say that the *conatus essendi* of the human ego must be included among material beings which, on the basis of the consistency and obstinacy of their inner cohesion and core-structure, remain fixed in their being, resisting all disintegration, giving them the character of *en soi* (**SA** 16). Even where it is a matter of splitting a single atom, the being in question (the atom) remains obstinate in its being, which accounts for its hardness and materiality. Physicists encounter this in the phenomenon of what they call "closure back into itself" (**VA** 92). All other modalities of life are likewise sealed in this same "urgency to be" (**AS** 32, 63). Think only of the plants that seem to want to grow everywhere and anywhere, pushing other plants aside, choking or smothering them so that they themselves can grow taller (**VA** 101). A look at the animal kingdom also confirms that this "attachment" to being as one's own being and life is nothing other than a *struggle for life*. This struggle is wild and merciless, leaving no place for ethics. Only the law of the strongest holds, and there is no question of responsibility and mutual respect. We also find this idea of a struggle for life in the thought of Darwin. Every living being fights for its life and survival, across the spectrum and grade of evolution: not only plants, but also animals, and no less so, humans who, biologically speaking, are the last stage in the evolution of animals (**PM** 172). To the degree that humans are driven by their biologically conditioned struggle to be, Levinas speaks of our "animality." He calls this the "instinctive ontology," which at the same time also implies the original or "natural axiology" of "inter-esse" as primordial value (**SA** 15-16).

This leads us to ask whether or not a human being is thus only an "exemplar" of Essence, and is at bottom simply like and equal to all other beings (matter, plants and animals). Without denying the ontological kinship between humans and all other beings, it remains necessary to insist that we not only belong to Essence, but are its most eminent exponent (though we will also see later how for Levinas this does not yet comprise the essential novelty of human being). In the human ego, Essence turns back toward itself, becomes self-conscious and complacent in itself, as it were "doubling" itself (**DVI** 78-79/43-45). Precisely as living and feeling effort to be, as aspiration and striving for freedom and self-development of itself—in short, as "ipseity"—the ego is the "sacrament" of Essence (**AE** 161-125); it is its ontological excellence (at least, to the degree that "ontological" features can be ascribed to the being of Essence) (**AS** 85). Initially, this "ipseity" is still pre-reflexive and lives thoughtlessly in a spontaneous and immediate folding back into itself, as *en soi*. Only afterward does it grow into conscious introspection, reflection, thematization and knowledge, as *pour soi* (as we will later see). As "excellent *gestalte*" of Essence, the human ego presents itself as "an interiority clothed in the essence of a personage, from a singularity taking pleasure in its ex-ception, concerned with its happiness—or with its salvation" (**DVI** 21/5).

The Ego as the Same Par Excellence

The attempt to further develop the ego as "ontological singularity" is aided, following an indication from Levinas himself (**AS** 29), by some useful points of departure set down in his first major work, *Totalité et Infini* (1961), where he characterizes the ego as "the Same" (*le Même*) par excellence (**TI** 6/36). Note that this identity is not an extrinsic but intrinsic identity (**TI** 198/222). The ego enacts itself as an identity which develops from inside out, and not from the outside in—not according to the definition of its character or by situating itself in a particular system of references. The ego is the same by proclaiming itself as itself, on its own initiative and without external help, in an effort and an attitude which we find expressed in everyday language, when one says, "as for me" (*quant à moi*) (**TI** 59/87). It is thus also on the basis of this intrinsic identity-structure that the ego manifests itself as a divide being, that is to say as irreducibly "separated" (**TI** 28/57) and accordingly in need of recognition and promotion. It is precisely this reaction to our structural dividedness and identity which gave rise to the classical vision of human rights as the right to autonomy and exercise of free will (**DAH** 43).

Now, this identity is not at all a static fact, but an exceptionally dynamic event or process of self-becoming (**TI** 6/36). The ego is not a being which always remains itself, or always tries to return, in tautological manner, to itself (in the form of 'A is A'), but one whose existence consists in identifying itself in and through everything it encounters (**DEHH** 166/89). In short, the identity of the ego accomplishes itself as a historical process of "self-identification." This brings us to the *quality* (the being *so*) of the *fact* (the being) of identity. The aim of identity is identity itself. The ego is its own objective (**TA** 140-141/152).

The Drama of Self-Becoming

At first sight, such an identical and self-identifying ego appears self-satisfied and self-assured. However, on closer inspection, it seems that this self-assurance is not without its own problems. Our freedom, and thus our responsibility in the first person, is not a safe and secure possession, but a "task," that is to say an ongoing conquest and a neverending effort. We are not free, but we become free—slowly, and not without exertion. To begin with, we are not yet fully ourselves: we are a desire to close the distance between us and ourselves—a desire to close the lack and fill in the emptiness we find within us. In its effort of being, the ego is in every way disturbed and thrown off balance. Its being is not neutral and placid, but animated by a tension expressing exceptional drama. "The identification of A as A is not a simple logical tautology, but the anxiety of A for A. The subjectivity of the subject is an identification of the same in its concern for itself" (**NP** 101).

The drama of the constitution of the ego is ultimately a matter of its finitude. As effort toward self-determination and self-development, the ego cannot forget that in its act of being there can be hiatuses, breaks, shortcomings and failures. The experience of falling short, of inadequacy to and for our task as human beings, experiences which remind us that we are unable to satisfy particular expectations, are a painful daily occurrence. Reacting to this, driven by a need to cancel it out, the ego is active only as free will, but not as "all-powerful." Its shortcomings grant it no peace, and often literally deprive it of sleep (**DVI** 79/44).

As finite—that is, mortal and limited—being, the "healthy" can not do otherwise than bind itself to its own being and from that self-concern strive toward self-determination and development (**AE** 222/ 176). Again, the ego is literally *pour soi*: it lives for itself, and in its anxiety about death it fights grimly and with all available means for its existence (**AE** 222/176). And this can hardly be cause for blame.

Within the tension of this process of self-becoming, Levinas distinguishes a negative and a positive dimension which, however, imply one another. Positively, the ego appears as growth toward autonomy and as struggle toward self-liberation. This already highlights the negative aspect of a break with all immersion or reduction, with every de-personalizing or alienating form of participation (**TI** 32/ 61): the ego is a real and free identity only if it exists from itself as an "interiority," and not from out of an all-embracing and all-consuming totality (**TI** 50/77).

The Ego as Original Freedom

According to Levinas' first independent works, *De l'existence à l'existant* (1947) and *Le temps et l'autre* (1947), the most threatening totality, the totality from which every other "totalitarian totality" is derived, is the "there is" (*il y a*): the anonymous, nocturnal chaos in which everything is reduced to "no-thing" (not something) and "no-one" (not someone), but without there being pure "nothingness." In the experience of the "there is," the ego is overpowered by the all-consuming mass of pure, undifferentiated being, through which it is "un-done" from itself. The ego can react to this brutal overwhelming by the "there is" only with "horror," with a trembling shrinking from the threat of imminent "de-subjectivization" (**EE** 93-95/57-58).

Levinas thus also describes the basic form of self-becoming as a "victory over the *there is*" (**TA** 140/52). And he calls this "first ontological experience" a necessary and functional step toward oneself as "self-sufficient" (**EPP** 122). The ego takes this first step by associating with and taking possession of its own being, through which it establishes itself as "here" and "now" (**EE** 117-126/69-73). "The ego emerges in its being in resistance to what destroys it" (**EPP** 122). Levinas designates this process with the technical philosophical term "hypostasis" (*hypostase*) (**TA** 132/43-44). The ego is and remains itself by repeatedly establishing itself in its being, localizing itself physically, and ceaselessly identifying with itself as the origin and endpoint of its own act of being. In this way, it tries to establish itself as principle or *archè*, understanding itself literally as an independent initiative departing from itself as "beginning," by pointing back to itself as "principle" and "origin" of its own exercise of being, but then finally returning back to itself as aim and endpoint of that exodus (**EE** 135-136/79-80). The specific identity of the ego lies in its intimacy with itself or its interiority. This has entered everyday language in reflective verb form: "it is not just that one *is*, one is *oneself*" (*on n'est pas, on s'est*) (**EE** 38/28).

The fact that the ego begins by itself, or rather always establishes itself anew as its own beginning and end, represents the deepest form of human "freedom." For the ego to exist in Levinas' sense of substance (hypostasis) is not so much for it to exist as such, as stable unity, as for it to persist in its act of being. It "is" in so far as it acts. Or again, it is not so much that the ego "is" as that it exists through taking up a relation with itself, with its being. It is in this restricted sense it is free, though this does not yet say anything about the concrete situation in which that freedom may or may not be exercised. This most basic freedom, in other words, is not yet the freedom of choice—not yet the freedom of insight, judgment and decision— but only the fundamental "freedom of the beginning" (**TA** 144/54). If we then cite the fact that this freedom is a primary condition enclosed in every human subject, we come upon the notion of *original* freedom such as the modern discourse on human rights has identified in its speech about a right to freedom and a right to exercise and concretize it as one sees fit. On this level, human rights express the absoluteness—taken literally: "ab-soluteness"—of every human being as free being. To stand up for human rights thus means to stand up for the emancipation of every human being from any reductive reference, as liberated from every determining order, both natural and social (**DHDA** 176).

For Levinas, this affirmation of original freedom implies not only the "fate" or fortune of the ego, but also immediately the "task" of responsibility (**EE** 136/79). This, then, is not a responsibility through and for the Other (as will be developed in my next chapter), but a responsibility for and from oneself. The ego takes its being on to itself, and indeed must do so. In this way, "being" is for the ego an assignment through which it becomes fully self-responsible. In the first instance, the ego can answer only for itself (**TA** 144-145/54-55). As "gravity of seriousness," this solitary responsibility also immediately implies "fatigue" as a consequence of the burden, and "indolence" (*la paresse*) as its anticipation: one is tired by the ceaseless labor against the bustle of existence, and one is sometimes loath to reassert oneself.

SELF-BECOMING AS ECONOMY

The inward movement of self-identification which Levinas calls the "hypostasis of the subject" remains only purely formal unless it is also mediated by objectivity. For the ego to determine itself as free and self-responsible identity, it does not suffice that it identify immediately with itself, for this would remain simply within the tautological circle of the "I am I." Looking solely into itself, the ego would find insufficient "material" or "content" to build up its freedom and identity. It always starts from lack of being (*manque d'être*), so that it has also always left itself in order to find itself.

Concretely, the hypostatic and thus physical ego needs the world in order to really come to itself and give itself real extension and quality (**TI** 7-8/37-38). In his description of this need, Levinas shows how the ego tries immediately to counter the threat that it implies. Precisely by refusing to resign itself to this need, the ego becomes a striving and desiring being: it becomes, in the strict sense of the word, an "effort" to be through which the dogmatic persistence that defines it unfolds into a "*being*-in the-world" (**AS** 64). As needy being, the ego lives in dependence on the world. Yet at the same time, it is in and through this dependence that it also gains its *in*dependence (**DEHH** 187/**Trace** 350). Driven by its neediness into the world, it tries to form an "answer" to it. "A need is return itself, the anxiety of the I for itself, egoism, original form of identification. It is the assimilating of the world in view of self-coincidence, in view of happiness" (**HAH** 45/94). In this sense, need is not purely negative. The ego finds escape in its needs; it is "happy" there. Neediness presents itself as a paradox: in the manner in which I experience my needs, there is on one hand dependence and on the other hand mastery—that is, mastery "in" this dependence. "Living from" (*vivre de*) the world is dependence reversed into sovereignty, into a happy affirmation of being. The shock flowing out of the negativity of needs is transformed into a source of liberation, self-establishment, fullness and "riches" (**TI** 87/114-115).

From this analysis of need, it emerges how the ego can realize itself as identity only when it raises itself up as lord and master of the world which responds and submits to that "ego-centrism." This essentially entails making the world "economically" useful. Levinas thus also defines the ego's effort of being as an "economy," in the most general sense of the word (**TI** 88/116). Broadly speaking, this economic relation with the world can also be described as "totalizing," as in the "economy of self-interest" (this use of "economy" will be further defined later). In order to defend itself against every all-consuming, de-personalizing or centrifugal totality, the ego makes itself the centerpoint of its own centripetal totality: the world is for the ego.

Practical Totalization

The totalizing ego first appears in its relation to the world as enjoyment, through which, thanks to a sort of naive, sheltered self-contraction it expresses itself to overflowing, protecting its fullness (**EPP** 122). Our first experience of the world is not by standing apart from it, as if it were an objective and ordered whole of separate things which may be indicated and used—*Zeuge*, as Heidegger would say—but occurs "in" and "of" that world. The world is first the "elemental world," the common milieu which, as a shoreless and embracing reality, implies within it all distinct "elements": earth, water, air, light and darkness, wind and clouds, sea and landscape... We are immersed in this elemental world. We are literally *in our element.*" We bathe in it and feel as at home in it as a fish in water. The elemental world does not merely surround us, but also runs through us, so that we are immanent to it, and participate in it from inside out. This "immersed participation" does not occur as if by conscious thought or reflective entry, but is the condition in which we always already find ourselves. The condition for the possibility of this "fluid existence" is "sensibility": sensible, or even sensual perception without the intervention of objectivizing reflection. This is the kernel of enjoyment. Participation in the elemental world goes together with a "sensible experience and living from oneself" as if born and sustained in the cosmic womb, which always involves a feeling of satisfaction and happiness (**TI** 81-116/109-142).

But the ego realizes very quickly that this enjoying self-satisfaction is also exposed to serious threat. It is stricken in the self-security of its identity by the unreliable indeterminacy of the elemental, which provides it with no definitive stability or security. The ego therefore tries to repel this emerging insecurity as much as possible by installing itself as master of everything around it, striving to make the world the ground and extension of its identity—that is, by making it into food and nourishment (**TI** 116-125/143-151). In this way, its effort of being evolves into a "grasping and digesting of being" (*saisie et digestion de l'être*) (**AS** 64).

Through this "practical" totalization, the ego strives to draw the world, as much as possible, into the circle of its existence, and then applies itself—often strenuously—to consolidate and even extend that circle as much as possible. This is possible only by reducing the other (whose sheer presence as other is disturbing) to oneself (**TI** 8/38), and by establishing oneself as the law and "measure of all things" (**TI** 30/59). The self-emancipating ego is necessarily allergic to the other, precisely on the ground of its effort to be, which manifests itself as relentless and unending struggle toward *self*-establishment and *self*-development in *self*-responsibility (**DEHH** 166/89).

According to Levinas, the fundamental modalities of this "economic or practical totalization" are dwelling, labor and possession (**TI** 125-158/152-183). At first, the ego does not entertain the question of its own dwelling, since the whole world is its home: in the elemental world, it is literally and figuratively "in its element." But, as we have already seen, the trustworthy elemental world in which I enjoy also exhibits an unpredictable strangeness in which there returns the threat of the "there is." This, of course, gives rise to feelings of insecurity and concern for the future. In response to this, the ego tries to conquer the negativity of the world by making for itself a home where it can feel secure and where it can return comfortably to itself. By creating within the walls of its own home a feeling of stability and intimacy, the ego is able to keep the unreliable world at a distance.

This may make it may seem that this dwelling is possible only through labor and the acquisition of property. However, it is not that these things make possible a dwelling, but in fact that the dwelling is their necessary condition. Consider first the matter of possession. Only by beginning from the dwelling, as worldly incarnated "turn inward," can the ego orient itself in the world sufficiently to then seek and make possessions. It can isolate certain elements of this world, and give them a place within the walls of its home, as "furniture." This furnishing of the home, that is to say the very act of dwelling, reinforces the ego's movement to itself. And since not everything can be taken into the home in this way, the ego must constantly try to extend its home with annexes or attachments: an enclosed garden, for example; a home village, town or city, if necessary, with walls; or home territory or fatherland, with well-defined borders, and so forth. In this way, it can be said that acquisition and possession tend to put to rest the uncertainty of the world. The movement driving one to possession now seems plainly egocentric, reductive and totalizing, directed to one's own safety and security, to the emergence, establishment and expansion of autonomous freedom, thus presenting itself not only as neediness, but also intolerant and even violent in its relation to a threatening world. Likewise, while the dynamic of acquisition and possession seems at first sight centrifugal in its self-overcoming toward the other, it now seems only centripetal in its aim at return to the self. It remains only a "half-transcendence," going out into the world only to return to itself in the immanence of self-interest. It is and it remains, in the literal sense of the word, "covetous" (**TI** 129-132/156-158).

Next and in the same line, consider labor. The acquisition of belongings, including even the dwelling itself, is impossible without labor. As operation and instrumentalization of the world, it is literally *en-ergy*: a "working-into" or working-on the world. This occurs preeminently with our hands. The handhold is the original form of technology, and has been extended and specialized in all sorts of instruments and machines through which the world can again be "handled," and can be reduced more and more to a form, service or function of the free self-affirmation of the ego (TI 131-140/158-166).

Noetic Totalization

A necessary condition for the possibility of this egocentric anthropocentrism, according to Levinas commonplace in the West, is the "comprehending knowledge" which always tries to reduce the other to the immanence of the same under the form of reducing him or her to oneself, as if the self is here and now the "master" of the world.

At first, the ego, free and happy in its enjoyment of the world, does not really reflect. Enjoyment can only happen "unreflectively," as a living of one's own life in the all-embracing comfort of the cosmic womb of the elemental world. Reflection becomes necessary when the ego feels itself threatened by the indeterminacy of the world and the uncertainty of its own future. This, as we have noted, makes it begin to feel concerned about itself, and in turn step back from itself in order to think about how it might respond to this threat to its happy effort of being.

Properly speaking, this reflection is not a kind of peaceful withdrawal to consider how one might solve this problem, leading then to a decision about how one might act to secure control over reality with a dwelling, possessions and labor. To the contrary, the ego moves immediately from its sense of insecurity into action, and it is in this action that reflection emerges as a means to help it. In the ego's inexperience, it displays an aggressive effort at a total grasp of the world which has the character of blind groping before it becomes self-assured. Lacking any "worldly knowledge," practical totalization feels amateurish, and thus still too much the pawn of chance and fate. The ego therefore looks for better means to solidify its position. This leads it to turn to knowledge as the means to pursuing a more methodical and systematic course in its economic concerns, so that it can return to its former mastery. Or better, in its more self-assured searching, there unfolds a measured and sophisticated insight which develops progressively into mature and structured objective knowledge (TI 114-115/140-142).

This inner combination of economic activity and objective knowledge flows from the fact that knowledge exhibits the same basic structure as does action: the reduction of the other to the same. In the act of knowing, the ego tries to undo the objective unruliness of the world by surprising it in those facets where it is accessible through "in-sight." Concretely, this occurs through conceptualization, categorization, thematization, systematization and *representation*, which is also to be understood as re-presentation of everything that had slipped away before, making it present and available again. The aim of all of this is to "com-*prehend*" (see also "con-*cept*"). By understanding the world, by "grasping" it, the ego can place it in the service of its own self-interested struggle to be, so that if it is at first dependent on the world, science and technology, as "grasping," immediately reverse that condition into an ever greater independence and "infinite freedom." To be sure, knowledge moves out of itself toward the other, but only with the aim of returning to itself "enriched" and stronger. The ego upholds itself precisely by "taking the other in hand," and "keeping it in hand" (think of the French *main*-tenance). Comprehensive knowledge aims finally at absoluteness (Hegel): it permits nothing to escape it, to remain outside it; it tries relentlessly and unsparingly to give everything a place, function or "meaning" within the world of its self-interest (**TI** 11-19/40-48). Comprehensive knowing is therefore far from neutral and innocent; to the contrary, it is a phenomenon of violence and power. It is a disrespectful and merciless "determination of the other by the same, without the same being determined by the other" (**TI** 145/170).

This comprehensive knowing expresses itself in language, in speech and writing, through which the intended object can be taken up into a story. Think, for example, of the encyclopedias and stories that are collected in our libraries, and through which we may thus read and understand both the present and the past as if masters of the world and its history. In this way, we in a certain sense qualify the otherness of the object. The source of its barbarian wildness—unconquerable and threatening—is undone, neutralized to an element of the horizon of meaning for a self-centered, thinking ego (**AE** 87-88/69-70).

FREEDOM AND HUMAN RIGHTS

In action and knowledge, which are comprehensive, we can see how the restlessness stimulated by a sense of need is only temporary and thus far from truly shaking the ego's identity with itself. By fighting against this economic insecurity, re-positioning itself in that economy and putting it in order, the ego immediately retrenches the security of its existence. Ultimately, it is unshakable in its conviction in favor of its *conatus essendi* and "use of good sense" in order to "overcome" its own limits and free itself of dependence on the world. But in doing so, its self-responsibility gives rise to a creative freedom which thereafter raises itself to ever greater freedom. As "means" and "possibility" exercised in thinking and doing, freedom necessarily manifests itself as a form of power over the other than oneself. Still, this power is in fact limited: we are finite, mortal beings, which means that we can not always reach everything we want. Yet, at the same time, freedom is an infinite desire for ever-greater power, fuelled by the secret hope for complete independence and mastery over all. The finitude of freedom means that it is tragic, but this does not change the fact that it always challenges its own limits, always trying to extend them. Freedom is experienced as an insatiable drive for growth and lust for expansion, a continuous effort to broaden one's own capacities and power (**TI** 55/83, 59/87).

This is true not only for liberation from strictly material needs, but also in the psychological-affective and existential domain, up to and including liberation from so-called "spiritual" needs. From its "hunger to be" (*appetit d'être*) (**SA** 15), the ego as it were comes from itself to an "economic religion" in which God is seen and considered as a "function" of the ego's totalizing autonomy. From its centripetal and economic concern with its own being, the ego proposes an "economic God" to intervene in human history from the height of a sovereign, infinite power. The ego itself creates a God after its own likeness, that is to say God as a "super-natural" and "extra-ordinary" power, "all-mighty" and therefore able to compensate the lack, or shortcomings in the ego's own effort to be. The terms "power" and "might," which are economic in nature, indicate how this divine intervention is seen as a constitutive part of a system of compensation and exchange built on, most deeply, the self-concern of the ego. Notwithstanding the fact that He transcends the world as *superpower*, and therefore can do everything that is for me impossible, still this God, precisely as *superpower*, is united to the world by the "unity of an economy" (**HAH** 38/89). This makes it clear how the term "supernatural" has no relation to an event that differs radically from the "natural dynamic of being," but to the contrary points to a qualitatively identical dynamic in a quantitative detour to, but also from the immanent power which animates us in our struggle for life. The facts that are licensed and made possible by such a God also come out in the consequences of all other powers and their intrigues. This is a God of magical powers that one asks for favors or "miracles." One can count on the interventions of such a supernatural and yet also immanent God. One might even try to exercise some influence on this God, just as one does with the other, worldly powers behind the events in one's life. The "fear of the Lord"—the awe, obedience, and love, the prayers and supplication, worship and honor coming to such a God—are all, says Levinas, nothing but the gratitude motivated by satisfaction, or more freely by a hungry belly (*une reconnaissance du ventre affamé*) (**AV** 119/95). In other words, the fear of God (*crainte de Dieu*) appears as a religious modality of the self-interested "fear for oneself" (*crainte pour soi*). One is prepared to honor God's commandments only so as to appease Him who, as the Almighty and Unfathomable, rules over our lives and decides our welfare. It is in fear and trembling that the ego puts itself in the service of God, hoping thus to receive "gifts" in return: it is not for nothing that we fear God (*Job* 1:9). Whatever the precise form which this economic idea of God receives in concrete religion, and however nuanced it may be, this basic economic dynamic remains the same. In one or another manner, God is taken up in the cycle of this economy, and the person asks more for himself than he realizes. It is a matter here of a "religion of needs" whose core is a sort of sacred egoism (**HAH** 38-39/89-90) remaining fully in the line of a "natural vitality" of the ego struggling toward freedom and well-being. However, such a religion is nonetheless indeed an expression of human reality in so far as the human being, in its savor for the sacred, recognizes that it is itself finite and therefore precisely *not* all-powerful. Still, since this God represents for this finite believer a key to what he himself can not attain, He remains a sign that, ultimately, the believer does not truly accept his finitude. And it is for exactly this reason that he falls back on God as function, correlate and extension of his self-interested effort to be. But then this God is no longer Holy, that is to say truly separated (*sanctus*: from *sancire*, to split or divide) and thus irreducible to the "being" of the ego and of all beings.

In summary, we can also say that the ego positions itself as, literally, *auto-nomous*: it considers itself the law, and not merely once, but continuously and progressively. Freedom understood structurally as separation is exercised dynamically as an endless striving toward identity. Freedom, in a manner of speaking, is the aim of freedom, understood now as free will: in its striving, freedom moves toward itself, and for itself, which is to say for its own "standing," and its development (**TI** 87-88/114-116). It is for the realization, maintenance and expansion of this freedom of the individual that, according to the classical vision of human rights (understood as right to freedom), there must be a guarantee, and this latter in a dynamic sense: we must promote a freedom which never has enough freedom (**DHDA** 179-182).

An Egocentric Model of Society

Let us now take up the interpersonal and socio-political aspect of the ego's economic-totalizing self-interest with regard to the world. As it struggles for autonomy and free self-development, the ego meets along its way not only the world but also other people. It therefore needs (to comprehend) not only the world, but also others if it is to be free and happy. In accordance with its "ontological nature" as effort to be, the ego is spontaneously inclined to extend its totalizing approach to the world to also enclose other people. It tries to draw the others into the project of its own existence, which is aimed first and always at freedom and liberation for itself. This leads to a self-interested, or egocentric model of society, grounded in the "economic, totalizing will to freedom" of the autonomous ego.

PRACTICAL AND NOETIC TOTALIZATION OF THE OTHER

Just is the case with regard to the ego's relation to the world, its relation to others exercises a reductiveness that is both practical and noetic. Here practical totalization is a matter of relating to the other person in a way which tries always to overpower or "functionalize" him or her. Concretely, it is a matter of "consumption"—of cannibalism with varying degrees of brutality (always in some way reducing the other to nourishment, sustenance). This can also take the form of "use," of making the other somehow subservient to the ego's own project of existence (reducing the other to an instrument) (**LC 268/CPP 20, TI 209/233**). Money is one "interesting" (!) means to do this. Money permits the ego to accumulate possessions and become rich, this also consolidating and expanding its independence: *liberté, indépendence de riche* (**SA** 16). And for those who do not succeed directly in becoming rich, money—whether pocket money or money in the bank—promises at least a temporary and precarious independence during the difficult years, days and hours of life. Money is thus not so much a ready tool for the establishment and development of one's own freedom, capacities and wealth—all with an eye to *l'en soi et pour soi*—but rather a nearly almighty instrument of power capable of guaranteeing everything else. It is in that sense that money is a form of practical totalization, and thus of violence toward others. The availability of money makes it possible to influence others and even to lay hold of them. Many people who have money think nothing at all of buying and selling others, because in our *conatus essendi* we are very tempted by the freedom and power which goes with money, or which it promises. The tyranny and cruelty of money are familiar enough in today's world (**SA** 16).

As for noetic totalization, we can speak of a "wild and autarchic thinking" which reduces the other to its "prey" (**AS** 63). This thinking carves its own path to the others and in the process undoes their difference and selfhood by submitting them to categories and concepts. However, one thus understands the others not merely according to oneself, but through a "horizon" which forms the basis for another "totality" (**TI** 265/289). From this horizon one surveys them in their individuality, but still takes hold of it as a 'that' or a 'what', through which they are no longer seen as this-individual-here-and-now but instead fall immediately within a general type or concept, an apriori idea, or an essence, whereupon they are located in a greater whole, structure or "order" (**TI** 16/44-45). More concretely, this means that those others who are seen from the perspective or path of the ego's thinking are seen only according to the wider horizon of their history, culture, environment, habits, characteristics, (depth-) psychological structures and social conditions (**QLT** 77/35-36). Here too, knowledge appears as power, or more specifically as power over one's fellow person. The ego's passage from distinct, separate individuals to a freedom obtained by means of the idea of others *in general* means not only that that ego understands them—no doubt in all innocence—but also that it takes them in hand, controls them, possesses them, suspending their freedom without actually depriving them of their real difference (**DEHH** 168/103).

RACISM AS DENIAL OF THE OTHER

In its extreme form, totalization can become, on the interpersonal level, a misunderstanding and even denial of the others—a phenomenon which Levinas considers to occur in its purest and most perverse form as racism (**VA** 100). Racism is the historical incarnation of the "diabolical criminality of absolute evil" (**CCH** 82) in the persecution of the Jews by National Socialism, which proclaimed itself the glorious, "apocalyptic" victor and believed with complete self-assurance in the achievement of eternity, beginning with a Thousand Year Reich (**AS** 60). For Levinas, the essence of racism consists in accepting only what is the "same," and excluding what is different, or "foreign." The "other" is found threatening and therefore ruled out. The only sort of otherness found acceptable is the otherness *within* one's own "genre" or "type"—the otherness within one's own blood or soil, one's own family, origin, nation, church, club or society, the same job, birthplace or birthdate. One accepts only differences and particularities within a same genre, which means that individuals within that genre differ only relatively (e.g., by character, taste and intellectual level). It also means that their deeper kinships relationships are not touched in any way by their differences (**VA** 97).

This makes it clear that, as has been attempted more than once, Hitlerian racism can not be explained away as a particular or even unique phenomenon which must not be compared to other, more familiar forms of violence. In order to hold ourselves apart from what emerges there, it happens all too often that we describe Hitlerism as something absolutely *unique*, having nothing to do with the ordinary struggle and actions of our everyday lives. Levinas' perspective allows us to see that Hitlerism and its genocidal crimes is only a quantitative expansion—that is, a consequent, systematic and inexorable expression—of racism in its pure form, which in turn is only a concretization of the *conatus essendi*: the ontological structure of human existence. No one is invulnerable to this perversion; everyone is potentially a racist. Hitlerism is not a chance event, an *accident de route*, but a permanent possibility woven into the "axiology of being" and our very ontological "nature." Those who follow only their own nature and live only their own lives, move inexorably toward the racism peaking in Hitlerism (**AS** 60-61).

We can find an illustration of this argument in the way Levinas interprets Heidegger's attraction to National Socialism (**CCH** 82-83). The fact that Heidegger believed in Hitler, if only for a moment (though, as Karl Löwith reports, this was a long moment), always remained for Levinas absolutely terrible, even excusing a certain "family influence" (Heidegger's wife was a very early follower of Hitler) (**EFP** 79). And to make matters worse, "the participation of this great philosopher in National Socialism is," writes Levinas, "a terror left unexplained by his philosophy" (**MPR** 19-20). In other words, there is nothing in Heidegger's "ontology" and his descriptions of *Dasein* as characterized by "comprehension" and "care" (*Sorge*), worked out so remarkably in the early pages of *Sein und Zeit* (1927), that plainly foreshadows National Socialist politics and its accompanying racist violence. As Levinas does not hesitate to say, those early pages testify to a powerful intellectual force and belong indisputably among the greatest texts of the whole of western philosophy (**MPR** 19). Along with Plato, Kant, Hegel and Bergson, Heidegger is in his estimation one of the five greatest philosophical geniuses the west has known (**EFP** 74).

Still, Levinas wonders whether we can be sure that the absolute evil which emerged in Hitlerism did not find an echo in Heidegger's *later* ontology: "The diabolical is not satisfied with the status of 'malicious,'" he warns us, "The diabolical is intelligent. It infiltrates wherever it wishes" (**CCH** 83). This infiltration can find its way into a thinking without being noticed. In this sense, the diabolical can take hold of a thinking without calling attention to its contagion. Thus, while there is no explicit connection between Heidegger's ontology and Hitlerian racism, one can not rule out the disturbing possibility of a hidden, unwilled but no less real affinity between the two. This connection will then have manifested itself openly in Heidegger's sympathy for National Socialism, expressed in his 1933 address as Rector of the university in Freiburg, and again three years later when he still wore the swastika at a meeting with Löwith in Rome—and this latter after and in spite of his alleged break with National Socialism and his resignation from the rectorship only a few months after the Rectoral Address. According to Levinas, this doubt about Heidegger's participation in Hitlerian thought grows to near-certainty when one looks next at his silence about the extermination camps of the *Endlösung*, or *Shoah*, in the 1966 interview with *Der Spiegel*, published after his death (**MPR** 20). In that interview, Heidegger does apologize for certain "human shortcomings" of his, visible for example in his failure to express his sympathies to Husserl's wife at the time of her husband's illness and then death. He also offers a political justification for his acceptance of the Rectorship, as an attempt to "save what could be saved" of the university's scientific rigor. And, after all, philosophers are not always (or perhaps not usually?) heroes. But what Levinas finds unacceptable is the fact that in all of this Heidegger still says nothing at all about the deathcamps and gas chambers, the monstrous climax of all the injustices perpetrated during the emergence, establishment and expansion of the Hitler regime. Perhaps all of the injustices prior to the exterminations can be ascribed to the inevitable political immorality of the "State's reason," no doubt aided by a great deal of thoughtless, politically inexperienced and misguided 'good intentions' (have not all nations at some point in their history perpetrated violences in just this way?). It is also unsurprising that many citizens living in fear for themselves under a totalitarian regime—deplorable caution, appearing more like (understandable?) cowardice—are prepared to make every manner of compromise and slavish accommodation, suspect alliance, purely opportunistic contact and relation, ambiguous explanation and dubious action, all of which can still be attributed in a certain sense to weakness and therefore granted some clemency. "But to remain calmly silent about the gas chambers and death camps, does this not testify—all poor excuses aside—to a mindset completely closed to all sensitivity and thus in agreement with the horrible?" (CCH 83) By remaining silent, one becomes susceptible to the cunning by which the diabolical impresses itself on thinking. "In order to refuse the diabolical, one must first refute it. It requires an intellectual effort to recognize it" (CCH 83). Anyone who remains unaware of it, who does not submit it to criticism, sooner or later becomes, in his or her own thinking, its victim and exponent. But the diabolical presents itself to thinking even and already in this very critical vigilance!

It remains the case then, that whomever studies the phenomenon of Hitlerism, even very critically, does so with a deep feeling of ambivalence, as if the act of concerning oneself with Hitlerism—however necessary—involves us with something we might better keep away from. For by reflecting on Hitlerism and its view of humanity, one grants it, no doubt unwillingly, the rank and value of philosophy, something which the absolute evil contained in the name "Hitler" certainly does not deserve. Levinas himself is no stranger to this ambivalence. Concerning a 1934 article entitled "Quelques réflexions sur la philosophie de l'hitlérisme" (IH 27-41), he once wrote to me: "I have never included this article in my bibliography. I consider it a mistake to have spoken of the philosophy of the devil—of course, this was before Auschwitz, but what does that matter?! There are words that one is ashamed to associated with."

THE DENIAL OF THE OTHER AS MURDER AND HATE

The denial of others which is rooted in the practical and noetic totalization belonging to the ego's *conatus essendi* emerges in full force in the elimination of the others. While murder is indeed the most radical and of course most plainly physical incarnation of this denial, it is not its *only* incarnation (**TI** 209/232-233).

"Murder" is manifest not only as a fact taking place once and for all, but also as a passion driven by a specific intentionality which annihilates the other. The "denial" involved in functionalization and "consumption" of the others remains only partial. In the "hold" that I exercise on them, I not only contest their independence but also determine and maintain them in their reality such that they are and remain "for me." Killing is radical: one does not dominate (acquire, use and possess), but annihilates others; one expels them from their being. Murder forsakes the other absolutely, and at every moment of "com-prehension": one will not admit the other into one's own project of existing, and instead rules the other out, as "too much" and "in the way." Murder manifests itself as the effort and the realization of a relentless drive for unlimited power: the ego does not seek "all *or* nothing" but "all *and* nothing." It raises itself up as "everything," so that the other must be reduced to "nothing" or "nobody," to a being-no-more in both the factual and the active sense of the word "is" (*être* is understood not formally, as "existence," but qualitatively, as *conatus essendi* and thus "possibility") (**TI** 172/197-198).

In this connection, Levinas points out how "hate" is a specific form of denial at once closely related to murder and in a certain sense even worse. Hate is a paradoxical form of denial in that it wants to reject or destroy the other completely, yet not completely. From its danger-ous, offensive height, hate wishes to humiliate and crush the other, but without annihilating him once and for all. On one hand, hate aims at making the other suffer, reducing him or her to pure passiv-ity. But on the other hand, hate would like the other to remain active in that passivity, so that he or she can testify to the hate. In stronger terms, hate wants the other person to not only undergo it but also suffer under it, which is the only way for hate to become visible, or evident. Only the suffering of the other reveals the annihilating power at work in hate. It is not precisely the death of the other that hate wishes most, but death as highest form of suffering. Whoever hates, wants to be the cause of the suffering of which the hated is to be proof. To cause the other to suffer hate is not simply to reduce her to an object, but on the contrary to forcefully imprison her in her subjectivity. Or, perhaps better, hate at one and the same time both objectifies the other and does not objectify her. In her suffering, the other person must realize her abuse, and so the subject remains a subject. The insatiable character of hate is defined by its desire for *both* objectification and the endurance of subjectivity. To satisfy this condition—to satisfy hate—is also to keep hate unsatisfied, since there is always more to hate. The other satisfies hate only by becoming an object, and yet the other is also never object enough, since hate requires not only her fall but also and at the same time sufficient spiritual well-being to testify to it. It is this that makes hate so absurd and vile. Hate would like the other to die but without directly killing her; it holds the other, still living, at the brink of death, with the result that the other provides, with her terrible pain, clear witness to its triumph (**TI** 216/239)!

The Will to Freedom as Source of Conflict and War

According to Levinas, the totalization at the basis of consumptive functionalization—the denial and rejection occurring in racism, murder and hate—is also the source of violence and conflict and even of total war. I am not the only one enamored with my own freedom, driven to extend and develop it on the ground of a right to that freedom (**DHBV** 58); there also others whom I meet in this world whom I quickly realize can not simply be passed by in the course of their own efforts to be and claims to freedom. All people are "egos" animated by the same desire from freedom and happiness and for ever more freedom and happiness. They all want to protect, develop and expand their own identity as much as possible. Hence, of course, is it inevitable that the "natural" egocentrism of one person in search of autonomy strikes up against the spontaneous expansion of the same egocentrism in an other person, or ego (*alter ego*). This is only one instance of a more general situation of conflict. The many egos sharing a single world can not all occupy its centerpoint completely and at once. On the basis of their independent ontological natures, or efforts to be, we can say that each tries with every possible means to rise above the others and to measure them according to its own perspective (**DEHH** 173/104). "We are," to borrow an expression of

Hobbes, "wolves to one another" (*homo homini lupus*) (**EFP** 118). Accordingly, there develops a struggle for power of all against all, war in the most general and total sense of the word (**AE** 5/4-5). "The violence of war is the extension of pure perseverance in being" (**VA** 98). This explains Levinas' assertion, paradoxical enough, that an unlimited and absolute exercise of human rights, understood as the right to freedom for every ego, is nonethless also the source of conflict, violence and war: "war of all against all coming forth out of human Rights" (**DAH** 44)!

In his description of the internal dynamic of war, Levinas indicates precisely how we are to understand this. The idea that war is an extension, on the plane of intersubjectivity, of the Darwinian struggle for existence (**AEG** 30), might give the impression that this war is only a quantitatively greater, but not a qualitatively different mode of totalization. In that case, violence would only be a stronger form of "labor," or practical (and noetic) manipulation of worldly things and power: "the use of things, labor, consists in finding a point from which one can gain control over a tool, and from which, on the basis of general laws to which it is submitted, it can be made to serve to the will of the laborer" (**LC** 268/19). Now, at first sight it would seem that violence is ruled by an analogous dynamic. War seems to rest on nothing other than an "antagonism of forces" each of which takes the measure of the other (**TI** 197/222). The violent ego seems not to enter into real relation with the other ego, to whom the violence is done. One behaves *as if* one were alone. The ego assesses its antagonist as a "force," a brute power set loose without name and undeserving of autonomy. Just as for the laborer there is nothing, strictly speaking, "extraordinary," so the violent ego tries to simply pass over the individuality of his counterpart or enemy, preferring to consider her as no more than a part of a totality, or an element of a general calculus to be recognized and mastered (**LC** 267-268/18-19).

To repeat: this comparison between violence and labor is somewhat misleading. The assailant does not simply behave as one "blind power" who may be overpowered by another, "greater power." Rather, there are differences and degrees in precisely how the assailing, violent ego relates to his antagonist. This is first a matter not merely of power against power, but of taking into account another freedom.

On second look, violence is more than a pure contest of powers which the strongest wins. The violent ego recognizes the fact that the antagonist also has a will. Violence is a relation between two freedoms taking stock of one another. And in this relation, numerous unforeseen conditions—for the victim and for the assailant—play an important role: courage, skill, self-sacrifice, ingenuity, cunning, creativity, and so forth (**DEHH** 168/103). The so-called "power" which the ego meets is of an unpredictable and inscrutable nature, for it is the "power" of a free antagonist. The other person does not blindly resist the violence of the ego, as do things, but freely, consciously and sometimes with careful deliberation. If the antagonist is free, then he or she also possesses all of the most effective means to bring down his or her aggressor. The violent ego is always at risk of having its tactics fail, since the enemy it faces can see through them, and perhaps manage to win the battle though superior tactics of its own. "No logistics guarantees victory. The calculations that make possible the determination of the outcome of a play of forces within a totality do not decide war. It lies at the boundary of a supreme confidence in oneself and an extreme risk." (**TI** 198/223). It is in this sense that war must be said to presuppose the freedom and difference of the other. The fact that the ego takes thorough account of the "inaccessibility" of the antagonist (through which its own best efforts, as aggressor, can be undone) indicates that the ego in fact does recognize the other in his or her freedom and difference, that is to say in his or her irreducibility to an all-embracing totality of which he or she would be only a single part or fulfill a single function. War is not a hunt, and not a struggle with a "natural element," but a calculated confrontation with an opponent which presents itself "from itself" as possessing a freedom and independence equal to that of the aggressor.

The aggressor will therefore try to avoid the antagonist's freedom. He will try to avoid a frontal confrontation with the unpredictable. Concretely, this means avoiding a direct meeting: "the weak must be intelligent." The attacking ego will thus avoid looking the other directly in the eyes or to approach him openly. Instead, he will look at him obliquely, and try to outflank him or take him by surprise. Violence takes the form of cunning and ambush, of indirect attack, or attack in disguise. With or without spies and detectives, it seeks the

the opponent's vulnerable spots, his "Achilles' heel," by which he can be brought down from behind or at least thrown off balance. This "indirect consideration" in fact testifies to a sort of "false security" which exploits the ambiguity of the other's freedom. As effort of being—as freedom not yet fully in possession of itself—the freedom of the other is therefore also a faculty and a power that has yet to confirm itself. The ego is thus not pure freedom and autonomy, but, as potential freedom, always nonetheless a "force" trying to realize itself while also "never force enough." It is this aspect of the other which allows the aggressing ego to direct itself primarily or even exclusively in terms of *power*. It is also this which allows the ego to act "as if" the other is not freedom at all, but only a wild, brute force to be mastered only by a still greater "counter-force." Because the attacking ego experiences the antagonist as a free being, he tries to overcome that freedom, to push it aside and forget it, to act "as if" it does not exist. In other words, this acting "as if," this rejection and avoidance of the other's freedom, is possible only if the ego has first recognized that other as a free being. To consider the other ego as a force which one wishes to overpower and repudiate, to use or even kill, is possible only under the form of first recognizing the other's freedom and then acting as if it were not there. The denial of the other person's freedom, on which is then based violence and war, presupposes recognizing that freedom, even if this is not true recognition but rather an instantaneous concession which one tries immediately to suppress. The inseparable connection between denial and recognition, of avoiding the other's freedom and reckoning with it, constitutes a living being out of the bad faith that underlies every interpersonal relationship (**LC** 268-269/19-20).

Tyranny and Enslavement

The question, then, is how we are to avoid or overcome this destructive violence of total war. What means are available to the subject striving for freedom and self-development so as not to go so far as this?

It is in this connection that Levinas points to "tyranny" (**LC** 268-269/18-19). If at first sight, tyranny might appear less violent and destructive than does waging war "on the living and the dead," a closer look reveals that this, too, is a hardened form of denial between persons, though not of the mutual or reciprocal sort as occurs whenever any two free subjects meet. In the course of its struggle for power, the ego can become despotic. In that case, it will try not so much to kill the others as to use them, or manipulate them, so as to deprive them, in one another manner, the possibility of exercising their autonomy and freedom. Persuasion, rhetoric, propaganda, seduction, cunning, diplomacy, moral pressure, torture and physical violence (or threats of them), brainwashing, intimidation and usury: all are means by which the despotic ego tries to gain control over the capacity of others to define their own lives, determine their own freedom and animate their own effort to be—driving them to an overriding concern with survival, protection, safety and peace (**TI** 42/70).

The fact that concrete freedom is an incarnated freedom makes it thoroughly bound up with the sensible, the passionate, the irrational and pulsional. In turn, this makes concrete freedom vulnerable, subject to influence and manipulation. And this means that the potential for corruption and cowardice belong to it essentially. In its concrete expression, human freedom is not all heroic but, to the contrary, far closer to "ludicrous." What Levinas calls the will's "status," or its "ontological regime"—the corporeality of freedom—constitutes its essential fallibility. It is through this fallibility that it can be compelled to certain actions, even violence. Wealth and threats alike can lead the will to sell not only its products but even its very self (**TI** 205-206/229-230). Referring to the post-war Nazi trials, Levinas argues "in the face of overproud metaphysical systems, that human freedom succumbs to physical suffering and mysticism. Provided that one accepts his own death, one could in the past (before the Nazis) call oneself free. But now (under the Nazis) physical torture, cold and hunger or discipline, things stronger than death, can break this freedom. Even in its final hiding-place, where freedom consoles itself for its powerlessness to act, and remains a free thought, the strange will penetrates and enslaves it" (**DL** 198/149-150).

This tyrannical penetration and seizure of freedom produces "victims" which are not only "slaves" but, in extreme cases, "enslaved souls." It is possible for one person to become so much under the control of another that he becomes that other person's slave. His freedom then comes to depend on that other. He no longer has a will of his own, and has lost freedom both of act and thought. In its consequent form, this means that even the "capacity" to obey a command—implied in freedom—is uprooted. There is only a degenerate heteronomy, the action out of "blind" obedience of a truly enslaved soul. And "blind" means, literally, obedience without any conception of what obedience is. The enslaved subject loses the experience of his autonomy *and* of his obedience. There is no longer any "consciousness" of obedience, but only an inner, irresistible "inclination" or "drivenness" to comply with the one, or ones, in power (**TI** 213-214/236-237). This inclination, which can develop (or mutate) into a masochistic "lust," is marked by an absolute submissiveness and compliance, an "extreme weakness" which everyday parlance we might refer to as "slavish dependence" or "stupid trust." Under fascism, this situation takes the form of trust for the sake of trust, sacrifice for the sake of sacrifice, and obedience for the sake of obedience (**DL** 197/179). The drive to submit becomes second nature. The subject is so thoroughly overwhelmed and in the grasp of someone else that he no longer has any sense of being overwhelmed and in that grasp. The enslaved soul no longer relates to a strange and unreasonable order like a slap in the face. The tyrannical ego thus no longer finds anyone opposing him, but only a mass of "material" without substantial core or resistance over which he can thus triumph to his heart's content. Love of the master occupies the slave so completely that he or she can no longer take any real distance from it. Terror of the dictator possesses him or her thoroughly: one can not see the terror because one sees *through* the terror, or from within it (**LC** 265-266/16-17).

The question here is whether such a tyrant-slave relationship is indeed universal and, if so, capable of lasting. It seems rather difficult—which is not to say completely impossible—for one subject to submit all the others, in their self-interested pursuit of freedom, to his own power. Many of those others will resist with remarkable stubbornness in the name of their own freedom and identity. Moreover, whatever mastery the despotic, totalitarian ego is truly able to acquire over the others, it is never sure to penetrate all the way, or permanently, to the innermost depths of each. "Slaves" are, and remain, free subjects, at least potentially and by "nature." Some will certainly keep inside a degree of reservation, while at the same time behaving outwardly as if fully willing to comply with the orders of their master. And even if the reduction to "enslaved soul" is apparently successful, the tyrant must always nonetheless keep watch over his slaves. The drive for freedom might well be extinguished, at least for the moment, but as principle and structure it never disappears. In the slave there is always the latent possibility of a nostalgia for his or her own freedom, for life as his or her own master, exercising his or her own freedom. Circumstances of excessive injustice or terror can easily reawaken from the depths a new consciousness of the drive for one's own freedom, which then leads to subversion of the tyrannical order, or active resistance to it.

In this way, it appears that sooner or later each one of us, hungry for our own freedom and self-determination, has the experience that we can not really do without that desire. By "nature," everyone stands up for himself and or herself for his or her own right to freedom, for his or her so-called "basic rights." The struggle for life and death is therefore ultimately inextinguishable. Even if it is sometimes inactive, still it can at any time reappear on the horizon, threatening the existing order with catastrophe. No one is impervious to that threat—not even the tyrant.

READINESS FOR PEACE AS COMPROMISE

It must therefore be asked how this situation of conflict, violence and total war can really be avoided without falling immediately into the tyrant-slave relation which reduces one person to the will of another. Such a solution is possible only by overcoming, or rather, limiting every form of hate, violence, slavery and war. Individual freedom consists precisely in recognizing and managing one's own susceptibility to lapses, weakness, cowardice and betrayal, in short in living with the fact that one is not heroic and not almighty (**DL** 198/ 150). Freedom is the consciousness not only of one's own possibilities, but also and above all of one's limits. As consciousness of one's own possible shortcomings, freedom can recognize the possibility of violence beforehand and then try to avoid or at least diminish it (**TI** 219/241-242). Freedom itself already entails the time necessary to prevent *un*freedom. It is there that one finds the true heroism of freedom. Consciousness means: to have the time, and to make the time to anticipate one's own susceptibility to begin hating, enslaving and participating in deadly violence, so that that susceptibility can be temporarily, or better, for an undetermined time—and best, for good—ruled out. Here, to anticipate the future thus does not mean to hasten its approach or to bring it closer, but simply to take some distance from the "not yet," so to feel it as a *possibility* and not something inevitable or irresistible. In this way, there can appear not one approaching "present" but several possible futures. In short, freedom becomes "postponement of execution" and healthy distance (**TI** 214/ 237). On the verge of partial violence or total violence, and of direct violence or indirect violence, of war and enslavement, the effort to be is shocked in its wild, naive self-evidence; it becomes "reasonable." Confronted with its own "vitalistic animality," the ego becomes an *animal rationale*.

Concretely, autonomous subjects are driven together by fear for the vulnerability of their own freedom and fear of the destructive inhumanity of everyone else's effort to be. It is fear of a "natural violence" never far away which leads them to make comparisons, formulate compromises and come to an understanding among themselves (**AE** 5/4). In order to make possible this suspension of violence and war, free subjects must first come together and propose that it be stopped and that "peace" begin.

The result of all of this is an "agreement" built on the compromises imposed on the impatience and intolerance of the effort to be, which will henceforth "use common sense" on the condition that everyone else also do so, with the result that everyone is therefore to be awarded (and judged) for a reasonable exercise of his or her freedom. Each person must be satisfied with the same amount of freedom we are willing to grant the others. One sometimes sees this idea enshrined in a negative formulation of the Golden Rule: whatever you would not have done unto you, see to it that you yourself do not do to others. He who does not begrudge the lowest among us their due, also need not fear becoming prey of the sly or brutal violence of others. In this way, my own most immediate self-interest—survival—leads me to take care of the concerns of others, and to accept for myself the limitations which that must imply. Out of nothing other than self-interest, I am willing to pay a price for my security; I am willing to surrender a portion of my rights and freedom, to become co-responsible for the happiness of others. In order to protect my rights and freedom, I set limits on how far I will pursue them, and on how much I will exercise them. The generosity with which I serve the interests and opportunities of the others is, more fundamentally, a calculated payment made in order to better safeguard my own interests and opportunities (**AS** 61).

One thus sees that for Levinas the compromise which institutes and maintains peace is built not of mutual good will but reciprocal fear and mistrust. Each free ego wants only to pay whatever price is necessary to avoid the threats which others pose to his or her own self-interested totalization. In other words, interpersonal agreements are in the first place "economic-utilitarian." And one wants, as much as is possible, to take more from the other and surrender less oneself. The sort of deliberations of conscience which this implies are therefore imbued with calculation and strategy. The peace thus established is a "reasonable peace," a reciprocal ordering of opposed forces in a relative balance of powers. As limitation and postponement of violence, this peace can consist of nothing more than negotiation (*do et des*), contract and non-aggression. In this way, the murderous self-interest of every free subject—striving for its own freedom and standing up for it wherever threatened—becomes mutually delimiting and thus viable. The ego recognizes not only its own free rights and "inter-esse" (*conatus essendi*), but also those of the others, with whom it tries to reach a certain balance and likemindedness. It is in this way that self-interest develops into informed self-interest. Every ego gives up its solipsistic, self-ruled pursuit of freedom and happiness, and concedes that others have an equal right to freedom and happiness. Through this ascesis and calculus—at once accepting certain limits and seeking compensation—one tries to present oneself as innocent, as if self-interest were in fact its contrary: selflessness (**AS** 61).

EGOCENTRISM AS GUARANTEE OF
GENERALIZED INFORMED SELF-INTEREST

Still, this is not yet enough to truly guarantee peace and security. If it should happen that a single self-interested subject finds it possible to withdraw from an established compromise or that there is no longer any cause to fear the others, so that it is once again possible to exploit another person without serious risk, one can be certain that he or she will do it. It would be naive to suppose otherwise, for after all it is only out of informed self-interest that limits were accepted in the first place. From the moment that an occasion presents itself, that self-interest will reassert itself as the real force of a subject's life.

In order for a free subject to "effectively" and "permanently" adopt a more limited, or milder form of egocentrism, it is necessary for there to be an exterior, "reasonable and general order"—one which is established in written laws, judiciary procedure, structures and institutions which possess not only the force of general consensus but also the authority to prescribe and enforce. In other words, there must be an "external and objective" instance which sustains and supports laws and institutions, and which can therefore appear sacrosanct. We meet such an "instance" in the socio-political order of the state (**LC** 266/16), which can take the form of a national state or a "united states," or even of an international political structure. Only the political structure of the state is in position to guarantee reasonable freedom and security (**TI** 219/241). Through the external socio-political order and the invincible power that one accords to laws and institutions, the free subject knows itself to be safe from despotism and tyranny in other free subjects. "Politics tends toward reciprocal recognition, toward equality; it insures happiness. And political law concludes and sanctions the struggle for this recognition" (**TI** 35/64).

According to Levinas, this political rationality which pretends to guarantee peace lies in the line of the whole of the western tradition that, since Ancient Greece, has taught us to think peace from out of the True (**PP** 339/161). The central problem for Greek philosophy is the multiplicity and violence that springs forth from there. The Greeks see the separation between the same and the other as the source of all opposition and thus all conflict, violence and war. And peace, they conclude, can come only from a resolution of every difference into a higher or deeper unity (think, for example, of the Platonic or neo-Platonic idea of the One). Now such a resolution is in reality a *reduction* of the most negative sort: a reduction of the other to the same. This unity in assimilation and reduction is realized preeminently in philosophy, defined as "love of wisdom," or the search for truth via insight and knowledge. Knowledge triumphs over the irrationality of *doxa*, or "opinion." It is in knowledge that all potential tyrants lie in wait to alienate us from our autonomy by gathering all differences and oppositions under a common denominator (**DEHH** 166/89-90). Knowledge abolishes the disorder of the divergent multiplicity of everything disparate and foreign by collecting it all into a single totality defined by an overarching order. Knowledge reconciles the other with the same by discovering its "essence" or "substance"—its likeness (*l'identique en chacun*) (**PP** 339/161)—so that the differences which cause violence are degraded to "accidents" and thus become incidental and unimportant (**TH** 91-92/13-14).

Applied to the opposition and conflict between individuals, this would mean that peace is achieved on the basis of knowledge, whose Logos insures the truth. In other words, human individuals would be human through their consciousness. In their conflictual difference, individual egos reach a consensus thanks to their obedience to a rational and universal truth exceeding their respective individuality and irrationality. Accordingly, they are each able to enter into agreeing without compulsion or being forced to renounce their freedom (**PP** 339/161). The particular of each ego raises itself up to the (literal) auto-*nomy* of freedom: one gives oneself the universal law (autos-nomos) that impresses itself on the ego without actually compelling obedience. The will becomes practical reason which, according to Kant, obeys the universality of the moral law. Yet in this way the good will of ethics is reduced to a rational principle, which implies that its specificity no longer lies in its goodness or badness per se, but in the rational universality of the maxim by which the will acts in accord with practical reason (**RA** 9). Through their rational obedience to the universal law, it is possible for individuals who defend different truths and therefore stand in opposition to nonetheless put an end to their conflict and assimilate. Free people gather and unify around ideas and values in which they recognize something universal and which, consequently, they elevate to a "law" of thinking now extended to the social domain. This is the case with political "law," which likewise rests on rational and universal truths, so that peace is constituted through obedience to the law, which is also to say agreement with a general truth thought to be the same for everyone. It must be said that no one is actually *compelled*—though, of course, it is required that each of us necessarily limit the otherwise arbitrary exercise of freedom. For in essence the idea is that obedience is also agreement with our deepest self, or "nature," with that agreement having the same definition, embracing the same general truth, in everyone. In this sense, the ego opens itself to a freedom provided— and even offered—by the state, institutions and politics (U 301-302).

Even in cases where one does not begin from the rationality of a general law, such as in ethical and political theories based on the principle of need, one nonetheless also comes eventually to some sort of universality which, according to our rationality or perhaps healthy understanding, we all reach but without giving up our freedom. In such cases, too, one finds a kind of reason as the principle of freedom: it is in assenting to a certain rule or idea that one preserves and makes true his or her freedom. And if one begins from the principle of personal gain ("good consists in what does me good"), one still arrives at the thought that it would be "better" for all of us to reach some sort of understanding and then share the necessary goods. There exist very sophisticated, sublime ethical theories which claim that informed self-interest leads to altruism. This path, which is precisely the path of a "deliberate" self-interest, leads inevitably to the development or realization of insights which in fact comprise yet another version of rational universality. Sharing with the other presupposes that I restrict the pursuit of advantages to myself. But at the same time, the primacy of that pursuit remains, for it is no longer seriously contested by others since, guided by reflection and insight, I myself have put it aside so as to allow the others to participate in the available goods (**RA** 9).

The Humanism of the Ego and Social Equality

According to Levinas, the aforementioned social orders in essence only extend the individual tendency to totalization into the socio-political domain. In all such cases, society is seen as the multiplicity of separate egos whose freedom must be insured as much as possible by the state or overarching international political structures, aimed at "the satisfaction of the needs of all, but without the freedom and happiness of others coming under compulsion" (**DL** 355/277). In this way, one accords to the other person the status of the ego: the ego is the prototype of the "essence" of humanity. Levinas has referred to this as the "humanism of the ego" (**HAH** 12-13, Avant-propos), and finds it throughout classical western humanism, especially since the dawn of the Renaissance and then the Enlightenment (**CVH** 179). The famous "respect for the human person" with which traditional humanism begins can easily be interpreted as an expression of the struggle for personal freedom, or of the movement for emancipation and human rights, which do not stop at viewing socio-political laws in function of the rights in question, but also, if necessary, move to declare them unbinding or bankrupt when it is thought that they no longer serve human freedom and the "revolution" that is to serve freedom and freedom alone (**DL** 355/277).

This humanism of the free ego thus also forms the basis for an egocentric "social equality" (**TH** 106-110/25-28). Every ego is the equal of the others, and therefore has his or her own specific rights and duties. The state and its socio-political structures are to guarantee their observation and realization (**TH** 93/14). Concretely, social equality is comprised of the balance and mutual delimitation of private and group self-interests. One begins from the conviction that each of us knows best and will always protect his or her own interests. This takes shape in a national and international system of justice which strives to insure that everyone has access to the same legal means to stand up for his or her own freedom and rights. The reference point for the construction of such a system is thus plainly the ego and its so-called basic right to exercise free will, from which all legal rights are derived. One establishes his or her own rights in order to then also—whether by compulsion or through the "equal rights" movement—recognize those same rights for the others, understood thus as other selves, as *alter egos*. In other words, the free ego and its own self-interests are the cornerstone for the rights of the others: "The right of the human being that must therefore be recognized is the right of the ego. The human being is considered as an ego or as a citizen—[but] never in his or her irreducible originality or alterity, to which there is no access through reversibility or symmetry" (**TH** 93/14). Hence are legal rights in a self-interested form of society the result of a compromise from which a "technique of social equilibrium is drawn, harmonizing antagonistic forces" (**AE** 202/159), whether on the economic, military-strategic, institutional, administrative, corporate or socio-political strata (**IRDH** 112).

EGOCENTRISM DOES NOT ADEQUATELY UNDERSTAND PEACE AND FREE RIGHTS

This does not mean that there is nothing positive and humanizing in the egocentric model of state and society. Armed peace is of course better than open war, and compromise is better than violence (**AE** 5/4-5). Social stipulations and legally sanctioned free rights are better than having to fight for one's own freedom and rights without regard for the others (**SA** 16). In these respects, we can certainly refer to the egocentric socio-political and juridical order as promoting, in a limited way, a "just state" (**LC** 266/17). Or, more precisely: "the necessity of providing for an order that insures freedom without tyranny constitutes the absolutely valid aspect of the political solution to the problem of the exercise of freedom" (**LC** 272/23). Referring to the Talmud, Levinas says that we must "pray for the state, for without it people would eat each other alive" (**TMD** 288).

ONLY FACTUAL LIMITS, NO PRINCIPLE OF PLACING ONESELF IN QUESTION

These last remarks do not take away from the fact that Levinas sharply criticizes the egocentric model of society as it interprets peace and human rights. This criticism applies above all to the very foundation and principle of this model of society. The move from conflict to "reconciliation," compromise and socio-political equality, inspired throughout by an egocentrism based on the "war of all against all," occurs without any radical alteration. "It does not resist interest"(**AE** 5/5). One remains enclosed in the "same"; nothing essential has changed; there is nothing new under the sun, notwithstanding the adaptations deemed necessary by and for our original effort to be. In other words, there is still no question of putting oneself (one's own interests) in question *as a matter of principle* and not merely by force of unavoidable or advantageous compromise. The self-interested to-talization of the ego has not yet been unmasked as "improper." The egocentric model of society goes no further than imposing external limits on what would otherwise be an unbridled exercise of the effort to be (**DEHH** 175/115-116). Conflict and violence are experienced as no more than expressions of unfortunate limits which, however, ask not for conversion but only temperance (**DEHH** 170/100). According to this theory, it is only out of uncertainty concerning the security and future of my own possibilities, or my own opportunities, only out of "fear and trembling" at the potentially superior power of the others who could then set restrictions on my freedom—or even cancel it entirely—thus only out of anxiety at the "war of all against all" that I am prepared to draw back on my megalomania, my unlimited lust for power and indulgence. This sort of "humility" only leads me to a moderation of my imperialistic drive for freedom, only to take account of reality, and to put some "order" in my relations with others. Everything remains permitted except what is impossible. And then, inevitably, failure and frustration emerge from the fact that I am not in position to realize my plans and ambitions, that I have not achieved complete success in developing my freedom. In violence and war I suffer from my failures and limited power, but without putting my *conatus essendi* fully into question. In a certain sense, of course, I do recognize the freedom of the other person—I do reckon with it in my very caution and insecurity—but this does not go so far as to abandon all interest in compensation or retribution (**DEHH** 168/96-97). The power of a stronger ego can indeed give pause to my freedom, impose limits on it or even rule it out entirely, but it can not bring the very exercise of my freedom into crisis so as to, as it were, unseat it. Shortcomings or limitations with respect to someone stronger is experienced only as weakness demanding better tactics on my part, but not as the expression of a "guilt" (*schuld*) requiring a personal, inner revolution (**TI** 56/84). I am prepared to make peace with the other person only on the condition that I myself can then live "in freedom and security." The confrontation with the self-interests of an other person thus does not radically change me, but only makes me more "sober": henceforth, I seek only what is truly accessible or available. One thinks of the popular wisdom expressed in the proverb, "Better a bird in the hand than ten in the bush." Such common sense is purely and simply a question of healthy understanding. At the core of my being, I do not feel shocked but only threatened. The egocentric orientation of my existence remains unchecked, even if it is the case that I can no longer pursue it without any limits whatsoever. And I accede to certain limits—not happily, but under the force of necessity—precisely in order to "save what can still be saved." Freedom does not yet comply with norms, but remains itself the norm" (**TI** 54/82). It is in this sense that Levinas contends that the politics built on the egocentric model of society is a "politics without ethics" (**AS** 61). After all, such a politics is in fact only an enlightened extension of ontological resoluteness and the Darwinian struggle for life, of which the freedom of the ego is said to be a refined, emancipatory expression.

According to Levinas, it is above all this essentially unchanged egocentric foundation for a number of very serious possibilities which makes it especially urgent that we recognize and pose for ourselves the question of a radical transcendence of the foregoing model of society. To begin with, it is clear how "reasonable" peace, as a sociopolitical extension of the rational form of an animal insistence on one's own effort to be—now bent on one's own rights and freedom—is only a very unstable peace, susceptible to great swings of power and shifting concentrations of interests. It is thus in fact an "armed peace" or even a "peaceful violence" (**MT** 367). This peace is not far at all from the "Cold War," with its muted, terrible patience—more patient than any direct attack—unseen beneath the surface of sociopolitical equality. So long as the will to power of the egocentric conception of freedom and individual rights is not put in question, we are not truly safe from a new struggle "to the death." It will always be conceivable, and possible, that new individuals or groups might try again to exert their influence and power with the aim of expanding their freedom. "As one free man alongside another, the ego is still the 'prince.' And even if the ego shares that sovereignty equally with others, he nonetheless remains in power: there remains the possibility of stoning other free people, of criminal enmity towards individuals, of violence exercised one upon the other, and suffered one at the hands of the others" (**MB** 71). This possibility, and the stability which it expresses, give rise, sooner or later, to the totalitarianism in which power rests in the hands of a single individual or group.

No Place for the Marginalized and Powerless

Furthermore—and this is at least as serious—the egocentric model of society also leads us to forget about the "marginalized" and powerless, who are defenseless and weak. For these people, it is not even possible to raise their plight as a cause for concern. This can be true not only of individuals, but also groups, entire nations or states, and even unions of states. Only the "privileged" and mighty count: only those whose "knowledge" and "abilities" make it possible for them to influence or control our perspective and priorities, whether interpersonal, social, economic or political. A society built of self-interest is necessarily a society built on egocentric relations of power worked out in a fluid balance of "forces." Accordingly, one takes account of the powerless only in so far as they (can) pose a "threat" to one's own position of power, the current balance of power, or the (generally disturbed) harmonious distribution of power. With a view to this assessment, Levinas contends that our western history has in fact been written only by its winners, and that our philosophy of history is often nothing more than a refection on the victories of those winners, hence forgetting the defeated, the victims, the persecuted, and the completely defenseless—both individuals and peoples. This he calls the "humanism of the proud"(**JG** 22)!

Levinas thus shows how violent resistance to violence, tyranny and war is ultimately no solution to them, notwithstanding a certain need for it. It remains only a "war against war" by which one continues to presuppose and start from the struggle for power between sub-jects no doubt enlightened as to their own nature but nonetheless still self-interested in their pursuit and defense of autonomy and the right to exercise their own freedom. The war of all against all testifies to a "wild humanity turned sober," jealously attached to the fulfill-ment of its being and surrounded with "military honors and virtues" (**AE** 233/185). Opposition to violence is not violence not yet put in question: one persists in violence oneself, now under the form of attempts to make oneself strongest or most cunning than the oth-ers—thus able to attain power solely by one's own efforts—but with-out for a moment questioning the force which all of this implies. Resistance to violence risks establishing new violence and a new form of courage, and new alienation and a new restriction of freedom (**DL** 368/287). "War against war prolongs war by doing away with its bad conscience" (**DL** 223-224/170-171).

Europe in Inner Contradiction

In this way, Levinas points out that all such perversions are not only possibilities always on the horizon but in fact realities which are the sad result of our western political history, built as it is on the idea of a universal rationality of which then state would be the primary in-carnation. Modernity, pride of Europe and triumph of reason, is also a time of reckoning and perilous balance. Witness the outcome of these past centuries of glorious discourse on knowledge, whose embodiment politics pretends to guarantee: lust for power, religious war, nationalism and totalitarianism, "political but nonetheless bloody fratricide, imperialism aimed at universality, human abuse and ex-ploitation, until in this century with its two world wars, its suppres-sion, genocide, holocaust, terrorism, unemployment, the endless misery of the third world, inexorable doctrines of fascism, national socialism, and the supreme paradox of the defense of the person en-veloped in Stalinism" (**U** 303). Hence did the so-called universal ra-tionality, on the basis of a universal truth which every freedom obeyed as if it were its deepest essence, only promise peace but in fact com-prise—and bring forth new forms of violence.

Another striking form of violence flowing from this universal political discourse was the imperialism of Europe and the "west." There has emerged, perhaps involuntarily, an identification between universality and Europe, which in turn has led directly to the idea of the centrality of Europe and the promotion of western hegemony. The concrete result of this development has been that European universalism tends to dismiss the particularity of other cultures as a "wild thinking" (Lévi-Strauss: *La pensée sauvage*) or "barbarian exoticism" which must be "raised up" to the level of "culture"—with this last word of course equated with *western* culture. In this way, universalizing—that is, western—discourse became the basis for colonialization of the third world, which was occupied, suppressed and exploited in the name of "civilization," all in response to an alleged vocation and duty to bring to others (**U** 303, **PP** 340/162).

Levinas thus calls us to recognize a contradiction in Europe itself, as the historical success of its rational principles become manifest in a manner opposed to the principles themselves. Great blocks of power exerting an ever greater influence on human destiny are themselves outgrowths of European politics, economy, science and technology, with all of their uncompromising, unvarying powers of expansion. These powers, now reaching far beyond the geographical frontiers of Europe itself, struggle so forcefully against one another for world hegemony that all of humanity and the earth itself are threatened with destruction many times over—and still they do not hesitate or withdraw from the battle, preferring instead to extend it beyond land and sea into the heavens, where nuclear strike tactics and strategies of prevention now ring the planet from above (**PP** 340-341/162-163).

THE BAD CONSCIENCE OF EUROPE

This contradiction turned back against Europe itself awakens in us Europeans a bad conscience. Europe no longer recognizes its own intentions in their results. And if this vision leaves behind a certain bitter aftertaste, it is not only due to disappointment or disillusion, but also the idea that the "dream" itself—of a universal rationality translated into politics—seems to have been a mistake. It is thus that Europe often appears weary: not so much from the pain it has suffered in a centuries-long struggle which seems to have ended far indeed from its original aspiration, as from a crisis centered on the fact that the principles of its project for a political rationality have contradicted themselves. Through the failure of its struggle for peace understood as stability and balance between (national and international) centers of power, and for human rights understood as the right to freedom, Europeans are now forced to question seriously the very basis of their own civilization. This question must be pressed explicitly to the alleged—or tacit—right of an expansionist *Wille zur Macht*, both in classical colonialism and neo-colonialism, as well as in international politics of terror (**ESC** 206-208).

A concrete incarnation of this bad conscience can be seen in the new values attributed to foreign cultures and civilizations no longer considered inferior but treated as equals. This development is underway not only in everyday life but also, and above all, in European universities, which have traditionally represented the peak of the universality of European discourse. Perhaps this latter expresses a remorseful attempt at reparations made to "other" cultures simply by attempting a philosophical and scientific reconsideration of the centrality of Europe (**PP** 340). There is also a sense of bad conscience at work in what are called the "new social movements" calling for a reinterpretation of human rights, peace, justice and our relation to the environment, challenging the old foundation of western society by attempting to replace it with something new and, again, "other."

Levinas uses the expression "full consciousness" to refer to this growing lucidity at our own contradictions comprising the bad conscience of Europe. He considers this a matter of the difference between a discourse moved by love of the wisdom consisting in objectifying (hence totalizing) knowledge and one moved instead by the "otherwise than being," or the call of the wisdom of love, which he understands as "responsibility-to-and-for-the-other." From this perspective, the crisis of Europe would seem to invoke the thought that Europe is not only and not even primarily Hellenic, and does not even rest primarily on Athens, but is based, or must be based at least as much on Jerusalem and the biblical tradition, in which it is the Torah, the wisdom of love, which grounds and also orients all thinking (**U** 303). With this thought, however, we have already entered into the concerns of the next chapter.

CHAPTER 3
PEACE AND HUMAN RIGHTS
BEGINNING FROM THE OTHER

All critical reflection on the concepts of justice, peace and human rights—carried out until now beginning from the ego—make it clear that we have not yet grasped their true nature. Bad conscience, which Levinas hears echoed in all such reflections, brings us to a fundamental question: are we wolves to one another (Hobbes) or our "brother's keeper" (Cain) (**EFP** 118)? Is war the "father of all" or are we committed to one another in peace? "It is of the greatest importance," writes Levinas, "to know whether state, society, law and power are necessary because a human is an animal to his or her fellow human (*homo homini lupus*), or because I am responsible for my neighbor. It is exceptionally important to know whether the political order marks out our responsibility or simply limits our animality" (**I** 137-138). In other words, does the socio-political, with its institutions, universal forms and establishments, settle on limits marking the consequences of human conflict, or flow from the contours of an infinite responsibility which reveals itself in the ethical relation (**EI** 85/80)? Are human rights, and consequently also the law, founded in the ego or the Other? Does their origin lie in the violence of self-interest or in the non-self-interestedness of goodness? Since Hobbes, all political philosophy would have it that what is meek and mild comes out of what is harsh and merciless (**ND** 58). Against this, Levinas asks whether "the egalitarian and just state, in which one is fulfilled (and which is to be set up, and especially to be maintained), proceeds from a war of all against all, or from the irreducible responsibility of the one for all, and if it can do without friendships and faces. It is not without importance to know that war does not become the instauration of a war in good conscience" (**AE** 202-203/159-160).

THE EPIPHANY OF THE FACE

Levinas clearly opts for responsibility-to-and-for-the-Other as the basis for a humane society. This is in no sense an arbitrary decision on his part, but rests on a strict philosophical analysis of the epiphany of the Face of the Other.

THE PRIMACY OF THE FACE-TO-FACE

Levinas directs this question to the "situation which precedes the law of the state as its necessary condition" (LC 267/18). This fundamental situation is, he says, the meeting of "face to face" in the direct I-Other relation. After all, he reasons, the establishment of a rational law and a political structure as guarantee of freedom "presupposes" that each individual subject enters freely into agreement with the others such that law and structure are indeed possible. But this entry into agreement presupposes in turn that these subjects speak to one another with a certain respect that is, in any event, without suppression. This "speech with one another" is essentially characterized by a directness whose absoluteness prompts Levinas to refer to the ethical relation where it occurs as the relation *par excellence* (LC 267/18, 270/21-22).

At this point, one might object that designating this direct relation of dialogue as primary or original without mediation can only be an attempt to conceptual evasion of the more apparently original situation of conflict in which subjects stand over against one another as rivals and enemies. To this, Levinas responds with a renewed analysis of violence and war, attempting to show that conflict is indeed secondary with respect to the meeting with a face precisely because it necessarily presupposes it: in a hidden way, the Good presides over the compromise of self-interested and yet rational peace (AE 5/4-5).

This response exemplifies the Husserlian inspiration for Levinas' method. Levinas steps back from what is more readily visible—in this case, the egocentric approach to freedom and peace—only to see through it *zu den Sachen selbst*, in the conviction that in that vision, as evident and plausible as it seems at first sight, the true essence of peace and human rights are "covered over" and forgotten, even excluded. Hence does Levinas also speak methodologically of a "reduction": what lies in plain evidence at hand must be unmasked and returned to its authentic, deeper meaning. In his writing, one finds repeated attempts to move beyond (*au-delà*), or better, before (*en-deçà*) in the sense of to the hither side, to the "underground" of the human subject, that is to say, under human freedom and self-interest, to a point where it appears that a human being is structured or "created" as an ethical "being to and for the Other," called to recognize the right of the Other. According to this ultimate structure where responsibility is anterior to freedom, the call to responsibility is therefore a call to be to-and-for all others, both near and far, present and future, as the final definition of a vocation to peace. But let us set this archaeology aside for the moment.

In the previous chapter, we saw how war can not be reduced to a pure antagonism of blind forces, but to the contrary seems already to presuppose the freedom of its protagonists. In retrospect, it now seems that there is in fact more involved than free subjects meeting one another. The fact that the power-hungry, imperialistic ego takes at least minimal account of the unpredictability of his or her adversary signifies that the ego has indeed recognized the other in its separateness and exteriority, which is to say, *as* Other, as a strange and incomprehensible presence which comes from elsewhere: "war involves a presence which always comes from elsewhere, a being that appears in a Face" (**TI** 198/222).

The same goes for the subterfuge by which war is frequently carried out. To watch one's adversary from an angle is not only an attempt to gain more power over him or her through cunning. It also expresses an attempt to avoid the other, to turn away from him so as to be able to treat him as pure force without any qualms of conscience. Again, this already implies the face-to-face encounter. I will have already recognized the other person as Other. If not, it is impossible to act as if he or she is simply an opposed power on which I can—brutally or subtly—vent myself. This acting "as if," this turn away from the Other, this aversion of my gaze from his or hers, is possible only if I have already looked the other in the face and thus already experienced as Other this one who asks for recognition as Other. To bluntly overtake the other, to use him or even kill him, is possible only by turning away from him and acting as if he is not an

Other deserving of respect. Denial of the Other necessarily presupposes recognition of the Other (**LC** 268-269/19-20).

With this, Levinas comes to the conclusion that all violence and war is preceded by—structurally, if not temporally—a situation in which two subjects stand eye-to-eye. The primary experience is that of an Other who turns directly to me. War is "can be produced only where discourse has been possible: discourse subtends war itself...Violence can aim only at a face" (**TI** 200/225). It is in this sense that Levinas can affirm that the *face-à-face* has an ultimate and fundamental meaning (**TI** 53/80-81, 196/221).

THE RADICAL ALTERITY OF THE OTHER

These conclusions require some clarification as to how the I-Other relation is not originally overpowering, reductive or totalizing, but rather peaceful or fundamentally without violence. In order to do so, we must enter more fully into Levinas' provocative phenomenology of the Face of the Other.

Concretely, the Other appears over against the totalizing effort to be, as a fact or givenness which resists the noetic and practical totalizations of the self-interested ego. In the process of affirming its own centrality in a world assembled around it, the ego is struck by this appearing precisely in so far as the Other appears as "radically other" (which is what Levinas has in mind when he capitalizes the word Other). Precisely where this Other escapes the concerns of the ego, Levinas speaks of the human Face.

What is initially striking in the encounter with the Other is his movement of "withdrawal" and "excess." The significance of the Other is secured neither in the horizon of the surrounding world, nor in evolution, history or any other system or totality. The Other exceeds every historical, sociological, psychological and cultural framework of meaning. How are we to understand such a transcendent alterity? The otherness of the Other does not consist in the fact that in comparison with me he proves to have certain features which typify him and not me. In everyday parlance, we tend to say that something is "other" because it has its own characteristics or properties, as for example where a white piece of paper is compared to a black one. We

distinguish each of these pieces of paper from the other because each
has its own properties and occupies a space other than that of its
counterpart. Where it is a matter of actions, people or situations, we
make such distinctions rather on the basis of different moments in
time. According to Levinas, none of this is yet the otherness which
distinguishes the Other person from me (**EFP** 95). It is not because
her hair is not like mine, has a different place in time than I, a different social position or different possessions, a specific character, aes-
thetic sensibility, intellectual level, psycho-affective structure—in
short, not because the facts in her passport are different than those in
mine—that the other person is radically Other (**VA** 97). These are
only relative othernesses, and not an ultimate or irreducible one. That
the Other is radically Other comes simply from the fact that she is
incomparable with anyone or anything else. The Other is precisely
her face because she is irreducible to an "exemplar," "case," "essence"
or "sort." Such a reduction would be at work in every instance of the
examples I have just given, all of which determine the individuality
of the person by referring it to a formal structure or locating it within
a certain type. This alterity would only be formal: the one is not the
other, regardless of what their respective content may be; each being
is other first with respect to each other being. Suppose there to be a
series of terms: a, b, c, d. A is other than b and b is other than a. Each
term in a same series is other with respect to each other, but all belong to the same genre, the same series. In this sense, they are not yet
radically different. In contrast, the other person does not belong to
any series or set: the otherness of the other person is not inscribed in
any logic and is not at all reversible or mutual. Properly speaking, the
other person exceeds and thus escapes the genre which is human. His
otherness is other than that of the series a, b, c, d. It is not relative but
absolute, and therefore wholly irreducible to either me or any genre.
The Other person is the unique, the singular and the exceptional par
excellence (**U** 301, 304-305). He is alone in his sort, or better, "outside every sort and every series," beyond every belonging, whether to
race, lineage, family or people—which already contains an indict-
ment of every form of racism (**VA** 98).

The Other is then also always infinitely more than the images,
representations and interpretations which I can and, of course, nec-

essarily do form of him. There can be no question of grasping him once and for all by identifying him with one or another plastic form (**EI** 90-91/86-87). Naturally, he does have his own specific physiognomy, with his own countenance and features, so that it is indeed possible, for instance, to photograph him. And he appears in a specific, for outsiders recognizable and identifiable manner, such that his facial expressions—and, by extension, relation to his body—permit a certain basic characterology and psychosomatics, from which one can no doubt deduce or at least hypothesize a great deal about his personality. But the face of the Other reveals itself precisely in breaking through its form and plastic image, in exceeding them and thus expressing the otherness of the Other as mystery (**TI** 126/152-153, **AE** 109/85). In this sense, it might well be better to prohibit photographs of the Other: to do so is to reduce the Other to what of him is visible, to fix him in his appearing at that single moment, in his appearance, and thus to reduce him to an object like all other objects (**EFP** 94). This amounts to depriving the Other of his face (*dé-visager*) (**AEG** 31). The face is really an "invisibility" which has already exceeded its visibility in the moment of epiphany. The face is "a being which surpasses every attribute. Through an attribute, it would be precisely qualified, that is, reduced to what it has in common with other beings; an attribute would make this being into a concept" (**MT** 369/**CPP** 39). The Other is essentially beyond every typology, characterology, diagnosis and classification, in short, every attempt to know and comprehend him. He makes all curiosity ridiculous (**TI** 46/74).

We might also call this phenomenology of the transcendence of the face an *anthropologica negativa*, referring of course to the *via negativa* or *theologica negativa* which responds iconoclastically to every concept or image of God, refusing or denying them in order to protect a sense of God's transcendence from what otherwise risks idolatry. Levinas' description of the face refuses assimilating it with a person's visible countenance in a way which parallels the biblical prohibition against fashioning representations of God (*l'interdit de la représentation*). According to Levinas, this parallel does not occur by chance: the ground for the biblical prohibition is not so much confessional and thus particular as it is philosophical and thus generally human. It implies denying the last word in thinking to imagination and conceptual knowledge, which we have already seen contributes to noetic totalization. Alterity is precisely the experience of a givenness which both submits itself to thinking and at the same time withdraws from it. Alterity—that of God and that of the Other—is that which makes appear the essential inadequacy of all attempts to think and understand it. It is that which makes itself available to thinking as unavailable, and thus never measurable by any thought: "un-thinkable" (**IRDH** 108).

Here there emerges a crucial difficulty raised by Jacques Derrida immediately after the appearance of *Totalité et Infini*, in 1961: Levinas, Derrida contended, seems to use Hegelian language in his own attempt to get free of Hegel. He would seem to define the Other precisely by contrasting it with the Same—a correlation which would in fact continue to imply the language of identity or, in Levinas' own locution, "sameness" (**PM** 179). Levinas' answer to this charge makes it clear that for him there exists only one language, whether it sides with Hegel or against him, and whether it evokes the Same or the Other. Arguing slightly *ad hominem*, he points out that Derrida's famous "deconstruction" can not legitimate or explain itself in deconstructed propositions, but only in the very sort of grammatical and conceptual constructions that deconstruction is dedicated to undoing. Nonetheless, the language of concept and representation does contain traces of difference and alterity. Levinas is thus of the judgment that conceptual and representational language includes the possibility of contesting both that which is said and that which perverts what is said through its own order and rules. The language which expresses the face and at the same time does injustice to it, is disposed—on ground of its own possibility—to also put itself in doubt, so that alterity is still revealed through language. In this way, Levinas can be seen to situate a kind of skepticism at the core of every philosophical thought and speech. This skepticism finds its true origin and foundation in the epiphany of the face which expresses itself and yet also puts that expression immediately in doubt. The essential ambiguity of a face at once appearing and withdrawing from that appearing is of a single piece with the constant ambiguity of language in thinking (**AS** 69-70).

Returning, then, to the description of the alterity of the face, we must now understand that the "unknown-ness" of the Other is not merely accidental or coincidental but essential and definitive. The conceptualizing ego will never be in a position to completely grasp and know the Other. The face is the site of what will forever remain "ungiven." It manifests itself paradoxically, as the "great unknown," or better, the "great unknowable." It appears in disappearing; it shows itself by withdrawing. The face leaves a trace by immediately disturbing its own trace, and even wiping it away. In this sense, it is the "inverted world" in so far as it will never be adequate to my presuppositions, apriori's and expectations. Completely unaccountable, it throws every prior description into confusion. It is a presence that immediately betrays itself—apostate or 'heretic' to itself. It is literally "extra-ordinary" and "e-normous," beyond every order and norm, the purest "anachronism," essential *enigma* (**AE** 109-115/86-91). Concretely, this implies that the Other is not constituted by me, as if satisfy or fill a lack in me, and even less as a mirror-image, another myself, or alter ego (**TA** 75/83-84).

THE EXPRESSION OF THE FACE IN WORD AND GAZE

This rather negative sketch of the otherness of the Other also implies a clearly positive meaning for it. The ground for its in-visibility, immeasurability and un-knowability is its *manifestation kath'auto* (**TI** 37/65). The face shows itself by breaking through all static and confining forms and images. It is precisely "expression" (**LC** 270/21). Concretely, this self-expression is fulfilled in the "word" and "gaze," or look, of the Face. The Face is that which looks me in the eye and addresses me (**DEHH** 173/105-106).

The Other is immediately present in its self-expression. I must not attempt any analogy which begins from the fact that the gaze or word come to me and concludes therefore that there is someone hidden behind that expression. The word and the gaze of the Other make her immediately present (**TI** 64-65/92). The primary, most fundamental content or message of this self-expression is nothing but the essential quality of the Other—her absolute otherness and irreducibility. It is not the *what* of the expression which is important here, but the *that*. The "fact" of her expression is the announcement of her very presence, her appearing "as" Other—which may also be the content of her expression (**TI** 170/196).

For this reason, Levinas designates the expression of the Other a "teaching" which, however, can in no way be assimilated with any form of (Socratic) maieutic. The expression of the face comes to me "from elsewhere" and brings me more than could be found within myself—namely, the real "message" or "revelation" of the presence of the Other (**TI** 22/51). The face does not awaken me to something already slumbering within, but teaches me something completely new: "The absolutely new is the Other [*Autrui*]" (**TI** 194/219). Such an Other is my "Teacher"; his very appearing instructs me magistrally about his irreducible altered, but without possibility of my having discovered that instruction myself, in the depths of my own soul. There can be no foreseeing or anticipating the revelatory word of the face. I do not have it already in hand in any sense. I am not the designer, but the imprisoned, the listening, the obedient (**TI** 41/69, 73/100).

RESPONSIBILITY IN THE SECOND PERSON

(BEGINNING FROM THE OTHER)

This "inexorability" with which the Face asserts itself into my existence is at the same time of an ethical nature: "the face is the fact that a being does not touch me in the 'indicative' but in the 'imperative'" (**LC** 270/21). In contrast with a common tendency in our day, Levinas has no aversion to the imperative—to what commands or orders us, to what bestows duty or requirement. Obedience is not ranked high in today's scale of values, and we do not easily submit ourselves to someone or something other. However, it would be a mistake to think that obedience is impossible without humiliation. One can obey without being enslaved. With the lack of prejudice proper to every true philosopher, Levinas does not hesitate to bring this out, stamping the initial structure of the face as an imperative. Of course, he also realizes that the imperative for human relations, as a human authority, can be deformed or perverted. It is certainly possible that it is not always the Good which voices a command. However, this is still not to say that every imperative is therefore issued from evil (**AS** 82). An ideological prejudice can make it impossible for us to discern the true bearing, ground and sense of the ethical imperative. Through his phenomenology of the face as imperative, Levinas wishes above all to clarify the primary positive meaning of the command as way to the Good.

The Face as Misery

The separateness and otherness of the Face manifests itself not only as inexorable and irreducible, but equally as "strangeness-destitution" *étrangeté-misère* and exceptional vulnerability (**TI** 47/75, 275/299). Since the Other comes absolutely "from elsewhere," she stands outside the horizon of the selfish ego's own secure world which, recall, refers first and only to that ego, or only to its neediness and finitude (even when it "reckons with" other people). Through its alterity, the Other is, as the Bible puts it, the "poor, stranger, widow and orphan" (**AS** 81): left completely to herself and to her fate, helpless, destitute, uprooted, homeless and in need of care, literally estranged. "The transcendence of the face is at the same time its absence from this world into which it enters... The strangeness that is freedom is also strangeness-as-misery.... The nakedness of his face extends into the nakedness of the body that is cold and that is ashamed of its nakedness. Existence *kath'auto* is, in the world, a destitution" (**TI** 47/75).

In our interaction with others we experience this helplessness each time anew, if in a refined—veiled and reserved—manner, for example in the expression "what can I do for you?" In this sense, it must be said that such a question, which departs from the very epiphany of the Other, does not always give clear expression to the misery of the Other, as would an actual helping hand reaching out to her. "The hand of Rodin—that is the face" (**AEG** 32). The face is not to be reduced to the physical countenance of the Other. The Face can express itself in a twisted back, where all the anxiety and doubt of a suffering soul are knotted in silence and yet unmistakable: *où la nuque devient visage* (**EFP** 134). To be sure, the Other can hide her face and disguise her poverty, as in the pretence to personal importance. But this posture disintegrates in its own appearance of holiness. The Other is more—or perhaps better: less—than his tie or jacket. As face, he is precisely that which is lain bare, and therefore can also always be humbled once again. Think, for example, of Solzhenitsyn's account of men who picked up others for interrogation (and internment) under Stalin, and, as a first humiliation, immediately cut the buttons off their pants. In this exceptionally painful event, the face of the Other is concretized for us (**AEG** 30, 33). The Face is not the great and fabulous, but the "persecuted truth" of "slaves in Egypt" (**CVH** 185). According to Levinas, the most eminent and at the same time most painful form of this miserable nakedness is our "mortality," of which physical pain is the menacing anticipation: "uprightness of exposition to death, without defenses" (*droiture d'une exposition à la mort, sans défense* (**DVI** 263/175). The mortality of the face is as inexorable as its direct and irreducible presence in its self-expression—to and with the merciless and inescapable paroxysm of dying in complete loneliness and indigence (**AR** 141-142).

THE FACE AS PROHIBITION: "YOU SHALL NOT KILL"

It is precisely through this essential weakness and vulnerability that the Face is "the temptation to murder" (**EI** 90/). Through its very appearing as naked otherness, thus as the powerless and needy poor, stranger, widow and orphan, the face as it were invites, or stronger, challenges the ego as it strives after happiness and greater power to now grasp the Other is his weakness. The face which is naked and mortal seduces me into reducing him to myself, leads me to acts of violence and even murder (**DVI** 244-245/161-163).

There is something remarkable at work in this seduction to violence. At the very moment that I am tempted to lay hold of an manipulate the Other in his weakness, I also realize that this, while factually possible, is nonetheless forbidden (**EPP** 124). Precisely this represents the core of the ethical. I am shocked in my self-satisfaction which urges itself ruthlessly forward. In the unprotected eyes of the face I discover myself to be his potential murderer. In this sense, I discover in the poverty of the Other a substantial strength, a radical resistance to my totalizing and reductive greed. The Face appears as "opposition": it stands over and "against" me and confronts me as a

radical "halt" or "no," as absolute resistance to all of my concerns
(**DEHH** 173/105). This resistance is in no sense coincidental or arbitrary. It rests not on some free choice by the Other, but on her
essential otherness itself, on a destitution which voices itself as match-
less protest against the ego's every reach toward it (**HS** 141).

The *logos* of this "no" is the prohibition "you shall not kill." The
content of this first wordless word of the face, this first speech anterior to any language, is thus specified by the murderous character we
have already witnessed in the ego's effort to be. This implies that the
fundamental word of the face has a dialectical structure: it presents
itself as "the negation of negation." This much we can be read in the
formulation of the prohibition itself: "you shall *not* [first negation]
kill [second negation]." The face confronts the imperialistic ego as a
"denial" of its movement of "denial" (*conatus essendi*). Levinas speaks
of the "im-possibility" of denial which is to be seen in the Other
person's eyes (**MT** 371/43). Of course, this is a matter of an ethical
"must not" or "may not," and not merely a "can not." Murderous
denial is always still possible. One need only consult the daily news-
paper reports of murder and mayhem to recognize that the sheer fact
of murder is indeed "banal" (**TI** 173/198). Levinas points beyond
this, to the "experience" that one can not remain indifferent to this
everyday fact. The face is, in other words, more than the neutral and
objective epiphany of irreducible altered and transcendence. It is not
so much a fact among many equivalent facts, one among many which
exist side-by-side and unaffected by one another. No, the face is the
remarkable fact that does something to me, that affects me and de-
neutralizes me. It does so precisely through the revelation of its transcendence as prohibition against destroying or denying it. This non-
neutral, non-indifferent fact is literally a wonder, or better the wonder par excellence.

Formulated positively, the double negation of the fundamental word
of the face implies a "duty" to respect and promote the Other in his
irreducible otherness—to do him justice in both his strength (irreducible unicity) and weakness (alienation-as-misery). This duty is
manifest in the radical asymmetry of the ego and the Other (**EPP**
123). Levinas refers to this as a "curvature of intersubjective space"
(**TI** 267/291). Through this prohibition against murder, the ego and

the Other are not only radically separated from one another, but also on different levels. This discrepancy depends not on the difference between their respective properties—not on any difference in their psychological dispositions and moods at the time of their meeting, and not on any difference in social status (**TI** 190/215)—but on the "ego-Other conjuncture" itself. Through its commanding character, the Other stands over me as a "law" bearing down on me from a "height" (*hauteur*) which is ethical. As such, the Other is not my equal but rather my "superior": not only my Teacher, revealing something radically new to me—namely, his irreducible alterity—but also my "Lord and master," who from an ethical height inspires me with awe, questioning me and laying hold of me unconditionally (**TI** 74-75/100-101).

The Disarming Authority of the Face

This affirmation of the face's absolute resistance to the murderous greed of the ego does not yet account for the full measure of its ethical significance. At this point, it would still be possible to interpret that resistance in terms of mutual "violence" between competing freedoms (as already described in Chapter 2). Were the Other to appear purely and simply as "freedom," as in-dependent and strong, then one would have to conclude that he is no more than a rival to the ego, caught up with him in a "struggle to the death." And thus would they come immediately into life-threatening conflict, where each would try with all possible means (whether straightforward or cunning) to overpower and reduce the other—resulting, then, in "war" in the most general sense (**VA** 98). Alongside this, it must also be asked how the imperative exteriority of the face is not "deadly," "crushing" the ego with a numinous menace instilling "fear and trembling" (**MT** 355/27). In other words, what makes the resistance of the face non-violent, or ethical?

It is precisely the "humility" of the Other, or rather her "humiliation," the "depth of suffering" where her altered truly lies, that the prohibition expressed in her face becomes ethical. As irreducible and obtrusive strangeness, the face does indeed "command" the ego's recognition and hospitality. But, deprived and destitute, she can not compel this from the ego—neither by physical force nor by moral persuasion. Through the fact that the Other in her physical vulnerability stands exposed not only to death but also murder, and thus can not assert herself as a power greater than the ego but must instead fall back to a *résistance quasi nulle*, she simply can not stand up to the ego as either opponent or obstacle. Hence does the Other not only appear as the ego's superior, but also commends herself essentially to its care. The face can therefore only "ask," or appeal to the ego for help in her misery. The powerlessness of her face renders an absolute command as the "please" of supplication. In his characteristically evocative, almost poetic style, Levinas speaks of the "timidity" of a face that "does not dare to dare." As first word, as word before all words, the face is a "request" not yet brutal enough to request anything, not yet courageous enough to "solicit" recognition and hospitality. It is a "beggar's request" that with bowed head and downcast eyes is uttered almost inaudibly, out of fear that it will be refused (**TI** 209/232-233). The face appears, in short, as a "disarming authority" (**AS** 33, 69). "What thus distinguishes the status of the face from every known object goes together with its contradictory character. It is, together and at the same time, both weakness and command." (**EPP** 124)

In this supplication, this beseechment which belongs to the essential alterity of the face itself, the command voiced there becomes specifically ethical in the full sense of the word. For a command is ethical only if it is directed to a free being, calling it to duty but without compelling or "convincing" it in any way, whether physically, emotionally, demagogically, diplomatically, financially, or through intimidation, bribery, blackmail or manipulation. Conversely, such a call for help is also ethical only if it is undeniable and unconditional, containing a "categorical imperative." If not, it is no more than a free-floating question, susceptible to a positive or negative response alike, depending on the discretion and mood of the person who hears it. The face, then, is ethical because it is both a command and a call for help, or better because it commands only insofar as it also calls for help (**TI** 48/75). This interwovenness of the command with the humility of supplication, the very core of ethical experience, Levinas condenses in the term *appèl*.

The Face Awakens Me to Responsibility and Peace

Initially, Levinas develops the significance of the face as ethical appeal as something negative and accusatory: in the face, I discover myself to be imperialistic and egocentric, possessed of a self-interest capable of murderous violence. This vision of my shamelessness fills me with a shame which is ethical. "Eye-to-eye" with the Other, I acquire a guilty conscience (HS 141-142/93-94). In the face, the Other appears as my "Judge," condemning me and placing me and my affairs radically in question (and not merely limiting them or suspending them momentarily). The Other manifests himself not as a compelling authority dooming my power and efforts to failure, but as someone whose "judgment" brings to crisis my naive "faith" that it is my right to exercise my effort to be straightforwardly and without concern elsewhere (HAH 74/132-133). "Is being just? Do I not kill by being? Do I truly have the right to be? Through my being in the world, do I not take the place of someone else? Do I not suppress the Other in my being and my thoughtless attempt to establish my effort to be?" (EI 129/120, 131/121) In this way, I stand under accusation by the face, so that my subjectivity reverts from the nominative "I" back into the accusative "me." I am no longer the principle (*archè*), the "measure of all things," but am myself placed in question and persecuted; I am the one who is "measured" (AE 140/109).

With this, we reach the principle being-in-question without which, according to Levinas, we cannot have relations and a society of peace. Before the appearing of the Other, my freedom is still naive and lacking any sense of guilt, still without any conception of its violent and warlike injustice. But in and through the appeal of the Other, that freedom is shocked in its credulity. In the face of the Other, it suddenly sees its selfishness and egoism; it feels a sense of guilt. Hence is a "conversion from inside out" possible—a catharsis of the wild and dogmatic effort to be (AS 64) through which the spiral of violence and war can at last really be broken (HAH 49/97).

The challenge to my naive and spontaneous claim to free self-development can not accurately be reduced to a negative event. More fundamentally, it is a call to responsibility for the Other (NP 107) which is likewise a commitment to peace with the Other, or better, whereby I am already "in peace" with the Other because responsibility brings me fraternal close to her in a bond of solidarity (**PP** 342/165). Every meeting between any two people begins with a blessing which is already contained in a common salutation, before the two even begin to speak. The good wish to be heard there goes much deeper, or much further (**AEG** 31). The simple and often unthinking, unexpressed greeting of the Other is the primary form of responsibility, manifesting attention and good intentions toward her. The French word on this occasion, *salut*, can also mean "salvation," and thus course evoke a connection with the holy, which for Levinas describes in marvelous fashion ethical responsibility. When I greet an Other, I wish him salvation—and that is always peace (**EPP** 122). For this reason, Levinas also describes responsibility or ethics as an essential form of "politeness": to put the Other before oneself. The good will in courtesy opens the way to the face (**EFP** 95).

What is immediately striking in all of this is that this responsibility which founds peace rests itself on an extreme heteronomy (**DEHH** 176/116). It does not originate from my initiative but goes always already ahead of my freedom (**AE** 12-13/10-11). In this sense, it can be considered *a priori* (**AS** 33). Through the appearing of the face, I am assigned my responsibility without being asked. It "happens" to me even before there could be any question of my choosing it. Levinas therefore also characterizes it as "an-archic" and "pre-original" (**AE** 12/10). It does not begin from my freedom, a freedom which establishes itself as *archè* and origin of all meaning, acting and responding thus in the first person only: responsibility has always already infiltrated my freedom from the outside and without my knowing it (**HAH** 74-75/133-134). The face literally "awakens" me to peace and solidarity: *éveil du moi par Autrui* (**NP** 12). It awakens in me the possibility—and at the same time the duty—to answer: "My responsibility rests on a complete passivity. Responsibility which is not yet a verbal answer, responsibility which is nothing but responsibility. One must take it in the form indicated by the French word ending with—*bilité*. A possibility to answer, a sensibility that is first speech" (**ND** 57). In this sense it is a responsibility "beginning from" the second person: "through (from) the Other" (**AE** 64/50).

All of this leads Levinas to describe the responsibility that founds peace as "the Other *in* the Same" (**AE** 32/25), or as ethical maternity, as "having the Other in one's skin" (**AE** 146/115). It begins traumatically, as extreme exposure and vulnerability to the face (**HAH** 91/145). It matures in being summoned to and taken hostage, or more positively, in being animated, motivated and inspired (**DVI** 33/13-14). The central category employed by Levinas in order to clarify this heteronomy and responsibility is "substitution" (**AE** 144/113). With this, he does not mean that the free ego actively puts itself in the place of the Other, but that it has already been put there— passively (**AE** 125-130/99-102). He also calls this the "creation" of the ethical subject (**AE** 140/110).

ELECTION TO THE PROMOTION OF PEACEFUL SOLIDARITY

This responsibility-through-and-for-the-Other immediately invokes the idea of "election" (**TI** 223/245). "The putting into question of the ego by the Other is ipso facto an election, an ordering to a privileged place on which everything depends but which is not at all an ego" (**NP** 108). The appeal of the face makes me personally responsible for the peace with the Other in which I already stand. Accordingly, I can not withdraw myself from that responsibility, since the face turns directly toward me and me alone—*face-à-face* (**DEHH** 196/**Trace** 353). Levinas refers to this as the "non-exchangeability" of responsibility (**HAH** 77/135). This also makes it clear how the heteronomy involved in responsibility for the Other does not imply alienation for me. While it does precede my freedom, this expresses a promotion to great height, or "messianic unicity" (**AE** 143/112). In election by the face I discover my unicity in a completely different manner than occurs in the struggle for identity in my effort to be. This unicity no longer falls back on my individuality, on my belonging to a sort of broader or wider concept of which I would be a particular example or exception (**CVH** 186). I am unique not because I differ from the others on the basis of my origin, kinship, race, social standing, perspective, profession, possessions and power, capacity or specialization, but because I am "singled out" as the only one chosen and called here and now to respond to this Other person.

In an irreducible way, the appeal of the face makes the Other "*my* affair" (**VA** 97-98). Far from denying me my freedom, responsibility in fact founds it or, as Levinas prefers to say, "invests" it (**DEHH** 176/116). As absolute passivity, responsibility reverts into irrecusibility, but one which is precisely entrusted to the initiative of a response (**DVI** 250/166). Only a free being is in a position to respond, but, through the election which always goes with responsibility for the Other, the freedom which this implies is at the same time also established (**TI** 223-224/245-246).

This idea of election also entails the idea of "fundamental option." It is impossible for me to simply withdraw from my responsibility (**HAH** 16/Avant-propos). I can not escape from the call of the face: I must answer (**DEHH** 195/**Trace** 352). *How* I answer depends on my freedom; *that* I answer does not. I must say "yes," but can say "no." The face places me inescapably before this choice: either reduce the Other person to a function, element or expression of my effort to be, or commit myself to her dire appeal (**TI** 191/215-216). He who refuses to choose for the latter commits Evil in the strictly ethical sense of the word: "Evil appears as sin, as responsibility despite itself precisely for refusing to take up its responsibility" (**HAH** 81/138). This refusal of responsibility—for which itself one is of course responsible—need not always be brutal and direct but can also conceal itself in subtlety, so that it might even appear courteous and refined. Concretely, this irresponsibility for which one is responsible can appear, for instance, under guise of the lighthearted frivolity of play (**NP** 76). Similarly, one might also try to escape from one's responsibility by withdrawing into pleasure, drink, drugs or eroticism (**AF** 222). "Absent-mindedness is evil" (**JR** 73). Contrarily, he who commits himself positively to the appeal of the face founds the Good, which is to say peace and solidarity (**HAH** 76-77/134-135). One takes one's responsibility upon oneself and declares oneself available: *me voici*—"Here I am" (**AE** 184/145).

A New Basis for Justice and Human Rights

From this redefinition of responsibility according to the appeal and recognition of the Other, Levinas can also redefine human rights.

Responsibility as Justice in the Broad Sense

For Levinas, the most fundamental dimension of a responsibility accepted and realized is "justice " in the broad sense of the term (**TI** 54/82). Especially in the period around the time of *Totalité et Infini*—though the argument never completely disappears—he even elevates this term over "love." In everyday language, this latter term is too often bound up with simple emotion, from which it can acquire an ambiguous and "seductive" character leading to all sorts of misuses (**AS** 77). To ascribe the establishment of peace in responsibility to love risks giving the impression that it comes out of a "feeling for the Other" rather than the unconditional command of the face. Many find it scandalous that love of neighbor (*caritas*) should be the content of a command: how can love be ordered? Surely, love can not be required!? Love flows from sympathy, heart, inclination.... Nevertheless, the biblical tradition considers it self-evident that love of neighbor is indeed commanded. According to Levinas, one finds the idea in Kant, too, when he forbids us to treat an other person as a means rather than an end in him or herself (**PZPR** 178-186). The command to responsibility coming to us in the face does not rest on some personal preference for just one Other person, on the ground of his or her (pleasant or interesting) qualities. This is not yet real love. The face commands us to respect the Other as Other, not according to any specific predilection but simply because that face orders me categorically. The rights of the Other come before my own, independent of any possible disposition or goodwill on my part. Justice as the Other's due is an absolute and inescapable command (**DL** 34/18). This is no philanthropy grounded in empathy and emotion, dependent on character or heart, but the ethically inescapable appeal to responsibility for the Other commanded by his or her face. Hence does it become clear how Levinas' concept of justice is indeed intended in the broad sense of the word, as doing justice to the Other, respecting him or her as Other and in this light promoting his or her concerns before one's own.

In this connection, it is not unimportant to point out how this sense of justice entails a form of knowledge or recognition completely apart from that of reductive comprehension. In *Totalité et Infini*, Levinas says that justice is prior to truth (**TI** 62/89). Concretely, this means that the speaking of the truth as the reproduction of something as it is in reality in fact presupposes the work of justice. Responsibility consists precisely in "letting be," in respecting, promoting and "recognizing" the Other person in his or her vulnerable strength. In this sense, doing right by the Other as Other, that is to say doing him or her justice, is also speaking the truth, or acting truthfully (correctly). Ethical recognition of the Other is also the source of commitment to the truth in our words and understanding.

This implies that scientific and technological knowledge can be transformed into a form of justice, of doing right by the Other and to the Other with the help of all of our scientific and technological enterprise. In this way, it can be said that science and technology are fundamentally "for the Other," and that justice is its "spirit." All too often they are simply handed over to the advances of reactionary social critique. Levinas does not ask "if" science and technology are responsible, but "how" or from what ethical sensitivity they are applied: from self-interest, which looks out only for itself, of from a sense of justice, which respects and promotes the Other as Other (**IS** 331).

The Ethical Basis of Justice and Human Rights

It is this fundamental justice, broadly speaking, which forms the direct basis for human rights, or better, represents the basic right on which rest all other rights, and thus human rights. The face hands me over to a responsibility that not only precedes "all limits for freedom and all war, on which according to Hegel history depends" (**DL** 34/18), but also every agreement or contract (**AE** 112/88-89). The appeal of the face thus also represents the first fundamental and minimal demand of right, namely the right to life, the right to respect for one's own otherness and history, for one's own personhood. To see a face is to hear: "You shall not kill." And to hear "You shall not kill" means "do justice to your neighbor and help him to live" (**IRDH** 111).

Justice therefore departs not from the empowered ego but from the disenfranchised Other: "the one whose rights we must defend is

primarily the Other person and not myself" (SaS 17/97). This brings
Levinas to propose further that the "human rights" which have become so well-known in our time are in fact originally and absolutely
the rights of the Other person. In a personal conversation with Levinas in Paris (October 6, 1985), he upheld the prophetic character of
standing up for human rights. From the moment this is integrated
by the State or institutionalized in structures of political power, it
risks losing its critical force, as we have already seen argued.

Through interpreting human rights beginning from the Other, it
becomes clear how responsibility is also the core of charity: "Everything begins with the rights of the Other and with my infinite responsibility" (JR 63). To love my neighbor is to respond to his Face,
to accept his ethical lordship over me and recognize that he has rights
over me (DL 186/139-140). A truly humane justice is thus possible
on the basis of a "humanism of the Other" which stands in contrast
with the classical humanism of the ego. The humanism of the Other
implies a de-throning and decentering of the ego: "There can be talk
of culture only when one reaches the conviction that the center of
my existence does not lie in myself" (CJ-I 31). "Resisting the idea
that existence is there 'for me' is not the same thing as resisting the
idea that it is there for humankind. Still less does it equal a rejection
of humanism or a departure from absoluteness and humanity. It is
one only through a denial that one's humanity comes in the place of
the ego. The human par excellence—the source of humanity—is the
Other" (TH 93/14).

Only when I raise the Other above myself is he or she no longer
considered a rival whose power must be put down, and instead as a
dignified person with unconditional right to recognition and treatment as Other. Hence is it now unmistakable that unselfish freedom
rests on the unconditional right of the Other as Other (IRDH 112).

At the same time, one also sees how ethical asymmetry also results
in an asymmetry on the level of human rights: justice begins as "heteronomy" and "inequality." It begins not in my freedom but in the
Other him or herself: it is "an-archic." Accordingly, the right of the
Other is primary with respect to the right of the ego. The Other is
not my equal but my superior, the one who teaches and commands
from a height which is ethical (TI 267/291). The right of the Other

is above my right. Levinas encapsulates this in the brutal statement: "the ego is the only one who has no rights" (**LPI** 50). The asymmetrical structure which this implies for basic human rights impresses itself on us in a very concrete ethical experience: what I must ask of myself is not to be compared with what I must ask of the Other. Conversely, then, the face may ask more of me than I may ask of the Other (**TI** 24/53). I know my duty to the Other and therefore ask of myself infinitely more than I do of the others (**DL** 39/22). I am responsible for the Other without being permitted to make claims on her responsibility for me (**HAH** 82/138-139, 99/150). I must take a further step out and away from all relations of reciprocity—and let there be no doubt, Levinas does not pretend that these do not exist between me and the Other—until realizing and accepting that I am responsible even for her responsibility (**AE** 106/85). I always have one more degree of responsibility (**EI** 105/98).

In this way, Levinas takes account of the thought that justice, or rather basic or fundamental human rights, originate in one or another physical, psychological, moral, economic or socio-political register. We have already seen how any power leads, by definition, to imperialism and violence. The only basis for a truly ethical justice is thus the unconditional responsibility announced to the ego in the appearing of the face.

None of this can be realized unless the ego accepts this responsibility as its own and takes it up—that is, breaks out of its unjust tendency to usurpation and permits the Other to experience "justice" (**DL** 187/140). A humane society is possible only on the basis of a law which takes the otherness of the Other as its first and deepest principle—only on the basis of a fundamental ethical relation of justice through which that otherness can indeed be recognized, and that recognition concretized (**SaS** 21/100). "In order for people to meet one another without conflict and in mutual recognition of each other's human dignity in which each is the equal of every other, 'it is necessary that one feel responsible for that equality,' a responsibility which goes so far that one renounces that equality for oneself and asks of oneself 'always more,' 'infinitely more.'" (**LPI** 50).

No Peace and Human Rights without Goodness

This demonstrates how justice and human rights can not be accomplished unless they are rooted in an unconditional willing-good-for-the-Other. In turn, it also leads Levinas to describe the content of the taking up of this responsibility-through-and-for-the-Other as "goodness." The call of the face awakens in me not only the seriousness of a guilty conscience, but also the desire to commit myself to the well-being of the Other in complete "dis-interestedness" (*dés-intéressément*), which is also to say to the human rights through which peace comes into being (**HAH** 46/94). Radical "diakonia," marked by the humility of one who has no time to look out for himself, who does not seek recognition or thanks, who acts not for his own salvation or personal immortality (which could still be called "egocentric"), but who takes the very destiny of the Other in his own shoulders to the point of self-denial and the self-sacrifice of suffering and even dying for the Other (**DEHH** 189-197/346-354). Levinas formulates this with the paradoxical statement that the truly ethical subject is to be recognized by the fact that she chooses to undergo injustice rather than commit it and fears her own death less than being the cause of the death of the Other (**TI** 222/244).

According to Levinas, it is in this unselfishness or goodness that appears what is really "new" in being human, or what is specific to humanity. Usually, such newness is located in human consciousness, thought, freedom and will, in short in the fact that a human is a rational animal (*animal rationale*). But since this rationality is nothing more than an extension of animality on to a higher level—a sophistication of the effort to be, the *struggle for life*—it is not yet anything really new. What is truly new or "extra-ordinary" emerges only when one's attachment to being is broken and abandoned. This takes precisely in and by humans, when one turns dis-inter-esse toward the Other, placing the Other's being and life before one's own (**AS** 32-33). Levinas calls this "otherwise than (selfish) being" (*autrement qu'être*) "the very miracle of the human in being" (**VA** 99).

Naturally, when compared with the healthy understanding of the effort of being, this unselfish goodness resembles pure folly, making humans look more like "irrational animals" (**PM** 172). But this folly, which does not measure or calculate but moves in a generosity beyond all self-concern or self-consciousness, is a very specific form of wisdom. It is the wisdom of love not to be confused with love of wisdom embodied in Greek philosophy, which wants to know and comprehend everything. It is the wisdom of learning to open oneself generously to the Other, rather than seeking to comprehend her, thus approaching her only with a grasp and gaze that returns everything to oneself (**AS** 64).

Levinas designates this newness holiness in so far as the ego recognizes the priority of the Other, permitting her to go first (*après vous*): "I believe that the human begins in holiness" (**PM** 172-173). This unselfish generosity is certainly not to be grasped quantitatively, in statistics; still less are all people saints or all saints always holy. But the eventuality of holiness, the fact that unselfishness as transcendence of being is possible, reveals the profound "grace" of human being in being. Such a grace can only awaken wonder, even if it does appear only rarely (**VA** 99): *for what little humanity adorns the earth.* All people understand the splendor of holiness; even those who contest it always do so in its name, or rather in the name of a greater holiness, a better goodness (**PM** 173).

Goodness as Economy of Given

Concretely, this goodness is enacted as mercy. When I stand eye to eye with the Other, I am called precisely *not* to hand the Other over to his fate but instead stand with him and by him. The destitution and nakedness of the Face implores and commands me to respond in mercy. This "mercy" is, according to Levinas, possibly only as the act of "giving" (**SA** 18). In no sense is it to be equated with or reduced to a sort of spiritual (and arbitrary) I-you friendship; in contrast, it must be a worldly, incarnated concern. For Levinas, true spirituality is animated not between purely spiritual beings, but beings which are also physical, or corporeal, and worldly. Human incarnation is the condition for the possibility of responsibility as goodness.

We must not respond to the epiphany of the Other as "poor, widow, orphan or stranger, disenfranchised, nomad or refugee" with pure emotion or sympathy. Levinas distinguishes "my hunger" from the "hunger of the Other." In certain spiritual movements concern for food, clothing, shelter, asylum and so forth is considered negatively as "materialistic." In the context of the selfish life of the ego this is of course correct. It is not so regarding the hunger of the Other person. But how is one to relate to the countless masses of poor and disenfranchised in the so-called underdeveloped world, if not according to this word "materialism"? We hear there the cry of a frustrated humanity. The ethical subject who takes seriously his responsibility for the Other will then also radically refuse to join those who call loudly (and suspiciously) for a unified front against that hunger, crusading in the name of spirituality against materialism. As if one is to form a front against a third world tortured by hunger! As if one ought to be thinking of anything else but satisfying that hunger! As if all the spirituality in the world would not be embodied in doing so! As if we in a collapsing world had other affairs to attend to than the suffering caused by the hunger of the Other person! "The hunger of someone else—terrible hunger, hunger for bread—is holy. The only bad materialism is our own" (**DL** 12/XIV).

Because the Other person is always unique and concrete, a person with real needs and desires all her own, the subject invested with responsibility must always answer her appeal very concretely—that is to say, "economically." The word "here I am" must literally become flesh. Whomever takes up his or her responsibility for the other must also take the Other's desires—her "inter-esse" seriously. In this sense, mercy is a very specific form of attachment to "being." It is not an attachment to one's own being, but "the positivity of an attachment to being as the being of the Other" (**SA** 18).

Note how this enriches the concept of economy. Within the framework of the effort to be, the economic is defined solely in terms of an egocentric-utilitarian relation to the world. Within the (infinitely) wider framework of unselfish goodness, it is clarified ethically, as the necessity of incarnating care for the Other. In this latter sense, the term "economy" is retained only very broadly. Later, we will see how the introduction of a third person—and other Other—reinstates it in a way closer to its more familiar meaning.

In any case, one sees now that the relation with the Other is not played out outside the world, according to a sort of beatific regard for her alterity, or "mystery," but only in and through the world. For not only the Other but also the ego is through and through physical, or corporeal, in character. Even though the ego in its economic total-ization is placed wholly in question by the face, still its response can never go so far as to completely surrender its attachment to the world. This means that the problem of feeding humanity—and each and every one of us suffers hunger on the basis of his or her own essential "strangeness-as-misery"—will be solved only if those of us in egocen-tric possession of the fruits of the earth cease looking on them as our rightful possessions and instead recognize that they are "gifts" for which we must first be thankful—gifts, then, to which the Other as Other has a right before we do (**SaS** 77/132). The ethical command going out from the naked face thus asks very concretely that I put my home and possessions, labor and knowledge, science and technology, in short my "dwelling" (*la demeure*), my established world, at the service of the Other. Mercy for the Other necessarily entails the worldly, material aspect of my "labor." It can not be satisfied with nothing more than sincere "compassion" or good intentions on the part of the subject. As the welcoming of the Other, as "response," mercy must offer the products of one's labor; mercy constitutes an ethically qualified economy (again, in the broad sense of the term). It is vain and hypocritical to turn empty-handed to the one in need: one must care for the Other with concrete goods. Regardless of the specific words or feelings which accompany the act, saying "you" must run through my entire body into my hands which carry gifts attending to your need. The hunger and need of the Other demand that I make unconditionally available to him every means and "dis-covery" of my scientific and technological know-how, putting them in the service of his well-being (**TI** 147-148/172-173).

According to Levinas, I must love my neighbor not only with "all my soul, all my heart and all my understanding," but also *all my money*. As we will see shortly, the concept of money receives its true meaning only with the appearance of the third person and the so-cially organized economy which thus becomes necessary. But when I meet this one Other person, here and now, it is my duty to feed him. At that moment, there is not yet an organized society—no shops, warehouses or banks. We are still alone together. Action is still a matter of straightforward, unqualified giving. In this sense, the level of mercy does not yet have need of money. And from the moment that there is indeed organized society and economy, with money playing a central role, that money becomes a "fact" and a "gift" which one can offer the Other in the same manner that one gives the tools one uses and the products one makes. Mercy thus admits no essential difference between giving money and giving food and drink: both expressions have the same basic (ethical) significance. Still, Levinas does observe that while it is relatively easy to give money, actually doing something for the Other—feeding him, clothing him, and above all rendering him hospitality in one's own home, sharing one's daily existence with him—these things cost much more (**NP** 54). The relative ease of giving money comes from the greater objectivity and distance which it affords as economic means, as compared to the immediacy of one's attachment to home and private property. Much more so than is the case with money, one's home and possessions are closely related to one's own ongoing effort to be.

A very specific and, according to Levinas, important form of "giving money," as one modality of the axiology of generosity, is "lending." As act of fraternity and mercy, the act of lending money must occur in complete gratuity, which excludes all reciprocity or *do ut des*. As modality of selfless giving, lending must not be contaminated by a sense of money as means of payment. This means that within the context of goodness lending can not be paired in any way with a demand for interest. While lending for interest is undoubtedly just on the level of organized society introduced by the presence of a third person, this is not so on the more fundamental level of initial fraternity. In the original and strict sense of the word, lending is an act of friendship and goodness. It is scandalous for a price to be set on goodness. As a matter of principle, there must be no demand for a reciprocal deed ("tit for tat"), compensation or remuneration. In no case may creaturely responsibility be reduced to a question of repayment!

Encountering the Suffering Other

For Levinas, the incarnated holiness of goodness in fact goes beyond giving. It must go all the way standing by the Other in her suffering and dying, which would thus represent the eminent and ultimate character of mercy.

Let us begin with the matter of suffering. In a forceful essay entitled "Useless Suffering" (1982), Levinas describes how suffering which is in essence always "wild and malicious," and therefore negative—up to and including its meaninglessness—is a concrete way in which the ethical appeal to responsibility may reach me. The Other's suffering (as, indeed, my own) is never "evil in general" but always extremely personal: it is the suffering of this one Other person, hence *her* suffering. The original and essential cruelty of suffering consists precisely there, in the fact that it never strikes humanity in the abstract, but always a very concrete, solitary individual who, moreover, is all the more solitary for being unable to escape this suffering, instead thrown back and enclosed within herself (**IS** 330-331). This is why suffering is so often manifest in a "cry," a complaint and protest by this one subject who must undergo this suffering, and who, precisely as subject (*sub-jectum*: literally, submitted to), finds it unbearable. To undergo pain is to weep and sigh, the basic form of non-verbal language (**EFP** 104-105).

As pain and lamentation, the suffering of the Other is a call for help, for care and companionship. In all its scandal, suffering exhibits a remarkable paradox. On one hand, it closes a person hopelessly within herself, throwing her completely back, inescapably, into her own body and self (**TA** 55/69). On the other hand, it is not a purely subjective experience, not completely solipsistic; the suffering person is no monad *without* doors and windows. To the contrary, the malice of suffering "for nothing" completes itself in a remarkable breakthrough. As closedness, there is no salvation to be found in suffering. This leaves the suffering Other no alternative but to break out of that enclosure, calling for help from other people—calling for companionship and aid external to the immanent structure of suffering as evil (**IS** 331). The malignancy of suffering manifests itself in a sigh, a cry, or a lamentation, that is to say in an openness outward,

aimed at someone else—at me—whose altered or exteriority promises salvation (aid). In this openness, the anthropological category of
the "medical" can not but emerge as primordially and irreducibly
ethical. In the immanence of suffering and above all of unbearable
pain, wholly unnecessary and absurd in its meaninglessness, there
flashes the transcendence of the "inter-human" (IS 331).

It is also on the ground of such suffering that physical care, and
indeed every form of care develop the technical competence visible
in the science of medicine. This signifies that the technique and technology of a medicine—or, for that matter, any other field—under-
pinned by medicine as physical care for the suffering Other can have
an essentially ethical basis and can be the expression of merciful responsibility through and for the Other person. Regardless of the degree to which (medical) technology slides easily into the so-called
"right-minded," conservative rigorism, still it flows not only, and not
even primarily or necessarily, from the willpower of the self-interested effort to be. According to Levinas, this bad will is simply the
price to be paid for a humane culture attuned by the face of the
Other to a call to feed the hungry and ease the suffering of the poor.
The manifest degeneration or abuse of (medical) technology is merely
the underside of its primary ethical significance, which consists in
concretizing attention to the suffering of the Other. The ethical basis
of medicine, and consequently also its norm, consists precisely in
being "through and for the suffering Other" (IS 332).

ACCOMPANYING THE DYING OTHER

In the sense that the Other person's inescapable suffering is an unmistakable announcement of her death, anticipated in the here and
now, the ethical goodness of heteronomous responsibility can be seen
to go all the way to accompanying her as she dies. "Fear for the Other"
or sympathy with her in her destiny implies that I can not be indifferent to her death, and even that her death is more important and
more painful than my own (AS 91). According to Levinas, this "fear
for the moral and dying Other" lies at the very basis of heteronomous responsibility. I am so affected by the death of the Other as to
have to answer for the ultimate violence which she, precisely as Other,

must suffer. Or better, the putting in question of my effort to be—marked with a Cain-like refusal to be my brother's keeper and, further, a temptation to kill him—*is already my responsibility* for the Other in the extreme vulnerability of her mortality: "an entry into the concern-for-the-death-of-the-other-man" (*entrée dans l'inquiétude-pour-la-mort-de-l'autre-homme*) (**DVI** 248/164). Concretely, the Other lays claim on me to stay with her as death looks her in the eye, even though there is ultimately nothing I can do against this inexorable enemy but answer "here I am" with freely-willed and sincerely concerned proximity, and "hold [her] hand" tightly, thus lightening her death and making it more bearable (**IS** 330-331). With the manifestation of the Other's death, the duty to offer her my hospitality, to meet her with open, giving hands (**AS** 76) becomes a duty to genuine goodness and pure charity "without greed and self-interest": it becomes a duty to non-indifference par excellence, one without any vestige of desire for returns, a non-reciprocal goodness which, compared with the inexorability of death, might even seem vain and conceited (**EI** 128/119).

Goodness as Desire

This unconditional goodness is characterized by a desire to reach ever greater heights of goodness. To the degree that I take up my responsibility for the needy, suffering and even dying Other, committing myself to the realization of her basic rights, there also grows in me the desire to achieve and build up ever more goodness. Grounded in and moved by the appeal going out from the unique Other, goodness can not but deepen into a veritable "art," ever more sharpened and refined, borne as it were by an "insatiable compassion," according to Dostoyevsky's remarkable formula in *Crime and Punishment* (**DEHH** 193/Trace 351).

Far from a subjective need or lack on the part of the ego, desire here is the fullness of a devotion and commitment which, however, is never devoted and committed enough: "proximity is never close enough" (*la proximité n'est jamais assez proche*) (**AE** 176-177/138-139). This desire continually deepens itself and fuels me with a hunger forever new. The commands that I set for myself grow. However much I take up my responsibility, I am that much more responsible. Levinas refers to this as the "infinition" of goodness. I can never again say "now this is enough, more is too much" (**HAH** 46-47/94-95). It is a lie for me to say "I have done my duty," for one is never in control of the ultimate situation of responsibility, never in control when it comes to the Other. I can never say no. Once I have met him, I am never done with him, even if it is true that, as one hears in the phrase "I've done all I can," we very often do indeed make an end to our responsibility. Aside the infinity which defines responsibility, what I have done—what I might well have just called "all I can do"—is very little, almost nothing. Because responsibility occurs very concretely, through the appeal voiced in the self-revelation of the Other person, the content of that responsibility is always new, always endless, always just beginning. In this sense, responsibility is always futural, not because it always still to come, but because it always does come (*qui n'est pas à venir, mais qui advient*) (**EPP** 125). My freedom is therefore also the *first* word taken from me, and not only the *last* word, taken by the realization of the heteronomous source of responsibility-to-and-for-the-Other (**NP** 63, 95).

Levinas also designates this self-infiniting or "living" infinity of gratuitous goodness as the "wonder of the Spirit." It is the fire fanned by, and burning, in its own flame. It is the genius of an unheard of discovery which also seems already conceived and accomplished. It is the love which burns without the beloved ever being satisfied, or without anything ever being truly given in return. It is the "good will" undertaken and accomplished despite the many obstacles threatening and impeding it. It is the restless commitment made in full cognizance of potential fiasco, failure, misunderstanding, mistake, refusal and even a simple lack of need—all of which permits Levinas to refer to this commitment as a "fine risk." This is the hope thrown out to the Other at the very moment (above all in suffering and dying) when all reason for hope seems to give way. It is a patience borne even under the fire of what can shatter it. The sources of its power and its reserves are infinite, so that in its creative urge the cautions of every strategic manoeuvre are exceeded. It forges cheerfully ahead without prior reckoning, lavishly engaged in the pursuit of the Other's rights, founding thus a peace with the Other which is never peaceful enough (**AE** 174-178/136-140). In contrast with the "mysticism of enthusiasm," which seems to take its criteria from the fervor and intensity of immersion in and fusion with its "object" (**DL** 47/28), Levinas refers to the infinition of goodness as a "mysticism of disenchantment" (**AR** 139). Goodness is not a romantic mix of happy feelings, but to the contrary the continual shock of a reawakening from which one must abandon and exceed oneself (**AR** 139).

Hearing a God Who Is Uncontaminated by Being

It would be a disservice to Levinas' vision of responsibility-to-and-for-the-Other for us to leave unexplored its religious depth or "under-ground." This must be contrasted with, above all, the functionalist interpretation of the idea of God which we have already examined. Doing so comprises the final passage of this chapter.

The foregoing serves to show how, according to Levinas, all speech about God is essentially situational. It occurs always in a specific existential-social context or conjuncture. There is no immediate access to God. The idea of God can only arise within our worldly situation. A thinking which would reach God as quickly and directly as possible is a cheap and naive thinking. A critical and mature thinking about God can speak sensibly only when it does not omit the intermediary stages supporting the word or call "God." The idea of God is a bridge which can not be built without scaffolding (**DVI** 8-9/xii-xiii). Hence does Levinas search the human context for the point at which God makes His entry, for the situation in which "God breaks in on us," such as is expressed in the title of one of his later works, *De Dieu qui vient à l'idée* (1982)—*Of God Who Comes to Mind.*

This implies that Levinas neither attempts in any way to prove the existence of God nor has any interest in developing a theology. To the contrary, his investigation operates on a level anterior and beyond that of any such proof or theology (**AE** 146/115). Still, he does take the view that the situation or conjuncture in which God breaks in on us does determine the quality of the respective idea of God. It is not that every context yields the same idea of God, and not that every idea of God has equal value. The content of an idea of God is directly and fundamentally conditioned by the nature of the soil from which it springs. Levinas thus seeks a God who is not contaminated by being, as he sometimes puts it. We have already encountered such a "contaminated God" as the extension of our self-interested effort to be, a "God" which is therefore "projected" or created in "our own image and likeness." According to Levinas, an *un*contaminated God, in whose image and likeness we ourselves are created, allows itself to be heard in the "otherwise than being" of responsibility-to-and-for-the-Other. The situation where God breaks in on us is, for Levinas, not the miracle or mystery of nature (it is not creation, but ethics which comes first). The "shock of the divine" happens primarily in the shattering of the immanent order of being which I can encompass in individual comprehension and make my own in individual capacity (**EFP** 93).

This breakthrough happens in the face. We have already seen how the altered of the face immediately evokes the ideas of separation, Height and elevation, and transcendence or the Holy—in short, the "divine" (**TI** 240/262-263). Through its self-revelation and teaching prior to my initiative, the Face calls up not only the idea of the creation of the ego, but also the idea of a God who passes radically before me. Through its "pre-original" and "an-archical" character with respect to the ego as origin and initiative, the Other resembles God, so that she "stands closer to God than I" (**DEHH** 174/106). For Levinas, it is thus clear: "the dimension of the divine opens forth from the human face" (**TI** 50/78).

To be sure, this does not mean that Levinas simply assimilates God with the human face. The alterity of the face "points" to God's transcendence, but without being its incarnation, symbol, or self-expression. Levinas even mentions the "disincarnation" of infinity, or "the" Infinite, in the finite inter-human face (**TI** 51/78). The manner in which the face points to God is that of the "trace" (*la trace*). The face points to God as Infinite as to the absent Third, the "He" (*Il*) in the "you" of the Face (*le Il au sein du* tu) (**ND** 56). Typical of the trace is that that which is left behind is not a presence: not the presence of what left something behind but the present absence, the absence now, of what passed by earlier. This notion of a trace is thus very different than that of Sherlock Holmes—or indeed, of us all, since we are all detectives. Holmes proceeded via a criminal's traces, some deductions, and reconstruction, until catching him. But if everything is ultimately deducible, the radical Other and the Infinite do not exist; there is no transcendence, no Other and also no God. If God is infinitely Other, he can have left in the Face of the Other person only a trace of what is irrecoverably past, never again to be retrieved (**AEG** 32-33). One thinks of Moses (*Ex* 33:18-23), who saw God only from behind, and after He had passed definitively by (**AS** 93-94). The face as a trace points to God as "He who has passed forever by" and who has withdrawn himself into an immemorial past (*passé immémorial*) (**AE** 123-127/96-101).

Levinas also refers to this as God's "anachoresis" (his self-withdrawal), or His "illeity" (He-ness as "over-there-ness"). In the face, we come upon the infinitely Other only in the trace as the "yonder," hence in the third person and not the second. This also implies that the Face, as trace of the Infinite, is always enigmatic and ambiguous, so that it remains invisible and incomprehensible. This enigma refers to a certain discretion in God's withdrawal and return (*récurrence*). The face is the manner in which the Infinite permits itself to be known without surrendering its reserve, or *incognito*. It presents itself as what does not present itself. We can also think of this as God's humility and *kenosis*, or self-differentiation. This self-humiliation is at the same time the way in which the "Glory" or divine transcendence of the Infinite "glori-fies" itself (**AE** 183-184/144-145). That this humble God withdraws infinitely deeper in the Face illustrates in paradoxical manner its goodness: God's withdrawal is also the exclusion from Himself of every pleasure. This is a goodness, then, which never seduces, impels, manipulates or forces itself upon us. Which in turn provides for a freedom and space where the recognition of God "can" (and not must) come entirely from humanity.

Let us note well: to establish God's transcendence and His non-thematizability in this way is not simply to conclude directly to negative theology (**AE** 14-15/17-18). It has as its positive correlate responsibility-to-and-for-the-Other, and as concretization of the "otherwise than being" it reveals the idea of God as qualified transcendence—as the idea of the infinite Good (**ND** 162).

In order to elucidate this de-formalized transcendence, we depart once again from the face, but now as ethical altered. Even if the face is only a trace of the Infinite, this trace is still an "impression" that the Infinite has left behind. This impression is wholly positive, unambiguous and above all unavoidable. The epiphany of the face is thus the command to responsibility for the Other person. This qualifies the idea of divine transcendence which breaks in on us in the face, as an *ethical* transcendence (**AR** 143-144). The trace that God has left behind in the word of the face is not so much language as an ethical word forbidding me to kill the Other and committing me to accompany her in attentive goodness, all the way to her suffering and death. According to Levinas, since the face is the ethical basis for human rights—primarily the rights of the Other person—human rights also constitute the juncture at which God breaks into human life, but without this comprising a proof for God's *existence* (**DHBV** 60). While the Other person is not the Infinite, in meeting his face I do hear the word of God, and this is no disengaged, neutral word but one which de-neutralizes me unconditionally, striking me to my very marrow.

This makes it clear how the kenosis and disincarnation of the Infinite in the (face of the) Other qualifies itself as an association with that Other as stranger, widow, orphan and poor. God's glorious transcendence consists, in other words, in descending from His majesty and aligns Himself with the suffering of the helpless and needy (**NP** 114-115). In so doing, He reveals Himself as the idea of the Good par excellence. But as the infinite Good, God does not remain external. Without losing His transcendence, He is nonetheless internal, or immanent. This flows from the responsibility expressed in confrontation with the Other. The appeal of the face does not remain external to me, but infiltrates me as an affection by the Other for the Other. In this sense, God's association with the Other—that is to say, His love—not at all a private affair between God and me. That God humbles Himself and binds Himself to the Other necessarily implies that He speaks directly to me from the Other and in the Other, as the command to love her (**PM** 176-177).

For Levinas, this makes it both possible and necessary to radically redefine God's omnipotence. God appears here no longer as a "super-natural" being of unsurpassed power, exceeding all worldly powers and supplementing the lack defining me as a finite being, but instead simply as the "helpless power" of the ethical appeal (**MPR** 17). This of course introduces a paradoxical concept of power, for the ethical appeal does not enable me to do anything as such but nonetheless does call me ineluctably out from myself. God is therefore to be described in no sense as weak, for this would mistakenly keep us within the categories of being, which privileges capacity, force, and strength. But according to Levinas, God is a matter for the "otherwise" than "nature," not a "more," which would still refer to "being" and thus the effort to be. God does indeed show His power in the Face, but this power is non-compelling: "disarming authority of the *Elohe Zebaoth*—the Lord of Hosts" (**AS** 85). This is also the God who, as almighty power, had remained silent at Auschwitz and who Nietzsche had already declared dead, but who at the same time has spoken in the ethical appeal and judgment which prohibits each of us from ever turning away from all violent, racist, and annihilating power, and commits us to stand up for the defenseless Face of the stranger. It is in the ethical appeal of the human Face that God irrupts as the "otherwise than being." (**AS** 81). This "other" God, who can not be proven by statistics and who emerges only as the very fact of humanity, *is* the protest against Auschwitz—not in the name of His power, but in the name of His authority (**AEG** 30-31).

If I commit myself to this disarming authority of the command, if I take up my responsibility, I also make effective the "otherwise than being" such that at the same time the transcendence of the Infinite is also realized, making it possible for the idea of the infinite Good to enter human lives. Hence is responsibility the intrigue of God's passing, or more strongly, His very life. Through the concrete fact of responsibility, the idea of the Good is more than purely an idea, but instead the distinct reality of the "spirit of the Good in me," possessing me, animating me, and compelling me to go out from myself and for the Other. As the infinite Good, God is my soul, the "more" in the "less," through which I continually overflow in a tireless, ever new, forever young commitment to the Other. In this sense, my being-to-the-Other is as much and as immediately a being-to-God (*être-à-Dieu*). In contrast with the self-interested religion of needs, we can speak here of a "religion of responsibility" (**DVI** 12/xiv).

As "beyond being," the conscientiously enacted responsibility-to-and-for-the-Other is ultimately also an inspired testimony, a "prophecy" of the Infinite. Where responsibility is fundamentally an unselfishness which is never unselfish enough—where it is a desire forever deepening itself—it makes present the "otherwise than being," not by reflection or predication but simply through concrete being and doing. In the "Here I am," I also express the Glory of the Infinite as the Good. Considering that this Glory shows itself precisely as infinite in the "infinition" of an ethical goodness full of desire (EI 114-116/105-107), it can not be singular or once and for all: through our ethical creation and the committed enactment of this creation, each and every one of us is an essential part of the epiphany of God in this world!

CHAPTER 4
PEACE AND SOCIAL, ECONOMIC, AND POLITICAL JUSTICE

According to Levinas, the foregoing account of "responsibility in the second person" is not yet the last word on our experience of heteronomous responsibility. By extension from the responsibility which comes to us from and through the Other (responsibility in the second person), there is yet another responsibility, which we might refer to as "responsibility in the third person." This dimension of responsibility becomes increasingly prominent especially in and after *Autrement qu'être ou au-delà de l'essence* (1974). This is so because it permits Levinas to extend his analysis of the interpersonal I-Other relation into the socio-political domain, at the same time valorizing the contribution of "Greek thought," by which he means the thinking that finds its source in Ancient Greece.

RESPONSIBILITY IN THE THIRD PERSON
(BEGINNING FROM THE "THIRD PARTY")
The Fact of the "Third Party" ("le tiers")

Levinas draws attention to this essential social dimension of the face by pointing immediately to an almost banal consideration: there is not only *one* Other person, but numerous Others. You and I are not alone together in this world, but share it with a great many. Moreover, these many Others are not always, and indeed usually not present to be seen or heard. And this is so not only in the spatial sense, but also temporally. There are not only other Others who are remote, but also future Others. This is why Levinas refers to them as "third parties": those to whom the ego, or first person "I," stands not in the direct relation of interlocutor to a second person "you," but instead in a relation to someone obliquely or indirectly present; as the third person "he" or "she," as "that one there," or "over there" (**AE** 20/17).

In his essay "The Ego and the Totality" (1954)—a text to which Levinas has attributed great importance for the way it assembles a number of diverse themes—the factual presence of the third person is approached through a phenomenology of what we commonly call "love." As a prototype of the I-you relation, love occurs on the level of experience as a "closed community." It takes place between "two" people committed exclusively to one another, and in that sense withdrawing from others in order to enjoy one another. It appears as an "intimate community" in which two people have chosen each other in such a way that their bond is permanent and definitive. For each of two lovers, being on love means being as if I and my beloved are alone in this world. They are alone together, and satisfied in one another. Each finds his or her fulfillment in the other, and both find in each other and in their relation the justification for their existence. The presence of the other is alone what counts, and comprises the sole content of the bond between them. This satisfaction comes from the emotional-affective warmth of tenderness and eventually passion (**MT** 358/30). According to Levinas, what is most important here is the fact that love is thus blind to the third person, to other others. And, since it always involves two people, it is in fact a blindness in complicity, the non-public par excellence (**TI** 242-243/264-265). This blindness, this lack of universality, "comes not from a shortage of generosity but the deepmost essence of love itself. Every form of love is—unless it becomes judge or justice—love of the couple. The closed community is the couple." (**MT** 360/32) But in this way, love is a denial of the factual structure of inter-human reality. In fact, an absolutely closed intimacy is never possible: the absent third is always a necessary disturbance there. Neither the "I" nor the "you," in the reciprocal exclusivity of their meaning and communication, are ever isolated beings but always stand in relation to others who are absent. More simply, these "third parties" are involuntarily excluded. Love would therefore be a veiled form of bad faith: one "knows" perfectly well that one must not exclude the third person, but nonetheless acts as if one can. A bond with the absent third person is thus always involved even in the intimacy of the I-you relation (**MT** 358/30).

Levinas further illustrates this irrecusibility of the third person with an analysis of the injustice that I can do the other person and the conditions necessary for its "pardon." It is commonly said that the evil we do is determined by the intentions guiding the act or acts in question. Now, according to Levinas, the conditions necessary for a genuine, legitimate and complete pardon can be realized only in intimate community where both partners are fully open to one another and thus in complete control of their actions. When in an intimate relation with the other I commit an injustice against him, this pardon is available to me only in the form of judgment of my actions made on the basis of a careful analysis of my intentions or examination of my conscience. Only after I thus confess my fault can the other person grant me forgiveness and forget what I have done. In this way, the relation with the other can free me from pain at actions escaping my will and intentions (**MT** 358-359/30-31). However, because, as we have just seen, that intimate relation is in fact an abstraction always involving an absent third person, the injustice which I have done the other person facing me here and now will also have consequences for other others. This makes plain the fact that the meaning of my actions does not always coincide with their intentions. The sense of an act goes beyond the intention alone: it acquires an "objective" significance which can not be enclosed within the life of the subject. My actions, then, can be unjust without my having intended it. Levinas refers to this as "social fault," and he describes it most concisely as follows: "The intention can not determine the action to its most distant consequences, and still the ego knows that it is responsible for them" (**MT** 360/32). What is proper to the social fault is that it can not be pardoned—not because it is too serious, but rather because it belongs to a different order than the pardon. With a social fault, the examination of conscience and analysis of intentions have no meaning. "I never intended this" is the vain excuse of an ego wishing to remain within the safe and comfortable circle of an intimate relation. An examination of one's explicit intentions can provide no assurance against the injustice visited on the absent third person (or to be visited on her in the future) by the actions in which those intentions are incarnated. The ego who commits this injustice can not own up to its unjustifiability because he has no knowledge of the injustice committed, and he is therefore unable to repay those who have had to suffer it. Moreover, it is also impossible for the ego to receive the other's forgiveness because that other does not know who has committed the offense (**MT** 357/29, 365/37). This brings us to what Levinas calls the "truly social": not the closed two-person I-you relation but the open relation between the ego and the Other wherein the third person is also an interlocutor.

THE UNIVERSALITY OF THE FACE

The entrance of the third person into the circle of the I-Other relation is neither by pure chance, nor a strictly empirical fact, but essentially bound up with the very appearing of the face. The You appearing in the epiphany of the face is not particular and privatized, but universal. The Other does not seek clandestine intimacy but places itself in the full light of revelation (**AE** 201/158). "Language, as presence of the face, does not invite complicity with the preferred being, the self-sufficient 'I-Thou' forgetful of the universe; in its frankness, it refuses the clandestinity of love, where it loses its frankness and meaning and turns into laughter or cooing. The third party looks at me in the eyes of the Other..." (**TI** 187-188 / TI 213).

This universality is founded on the very essence of the face, which is t say its radical alterity. As we have already seen, the naked face reveals both the exacting command of the Other and her imploring misery, or better: the exacting command *of* that misery. This points to a radical "equality" between all people, since each and all of us share in that radical (metaphysical) and ethical nakedness. In the self-expression of the face, according to Levinas' frequent formula, it is a matter not of the quantitative properties by which people resemble and differ from one another, but of the fundamental status of the human person *as* Other. The nakedness of the face consists in its unconditional expression, through secondary and contingent attributes, of the immediate presence of the Other. In the face, I experience the direct presence of "someone" else: an other person, or rather an Other as Other, which is to say as radically separate and distinct from me and therefore completely unique (**TH** 109-110/25-26).

Paradoxically enough, this point of uniqueness is also the point at which the Other can be said to appear universally, as the expression of all Others: when I meet the naked face of this one Other here and now, thus radically separate and distinct, I am also confronted with all Others, who call to me just humbly and with just as much imperative as does this one Other standing before me. In reality, my relation with the Other is thus never a relation with just one individual person: the third person is present "in" this second person Other from the very beginning. While the face represents the third as absent, it also nonetheless—indeed, by that same token—evokes her as present (i.e., present as absent). In the appearing of the Other, the third, too, already looks at me (**DVI** 132/82). "In the proximity of the Other, all the Others than the Other obsess me" (**AE** 201/158). Or again, as Levinas has put it already in *Totalité et Infini*: "The epiphany of the face qua face opens up humanity....The presence of the face, the infinity of the Other, is a destituteness, a presence of the third (that is, of the whole of humanity which looks at us" (**TI** 188/213). In this sense, the face is at once near and far, the present Other and the absent Other.

It is for this reason that Levinas never uses Buber's category of the "I-Thou" relation (**EFP** 123-124), but designates the I-Other relation as the "social relation" (**TI** 81/109) or simply as "sociality" (**AE** 33/26). The otherness of the Other has an essentially social extension: his alterity contains an immediate reference to all Others. Hence is "the Other from the first the brother of all other men" (**AE** 201/158). It seems, then, that our "universal kinship" is neither biological nor "generic"—it does not derive from some common quality or qualities—but of an ethical-metaphysical structure or character. This implies that racial kinship is not true proximity or kinship because it does not yet involve a closeness to the otherness of the Other who radically transcends individual identity. As a basis for identification, race refers everything to 'likenesses' or 'sameness'—to one's own race, one's own people, and one's own blood—so that the 'others', those who do not belong to my race, people, or blood, are excluded all the way, if necessary, to the point of denial and even annihilation (**AS**

61). In contrast, a truly humane kinship includes all Others precisely on the basis of their otherness and difference, as expressed in the face. This kinship thus also manifests itself as the creaturely *ur*-condition of a solidarity, 'fellowship' and connectedness in which the ego and all Others are, without any precondition or exception, placed together and so strongly bound to one another that each is *radically* (i.e., before every conscious engagement) committed to every Other in an inescapable and unconditional way (**AE** 178-179/139-140).

It is immediately clear how what we might now call *the universality of the face* has important consequences for what we have already described as heteronomous responsibility. If the face expresses to me the immediate and essential presence of all Others, then I in my responsibility for this Other here and now am also and at the same time unconditionally responsible for all Others. My responsibility has a universal scope. It is not only qualitatively infinite, because there is nothing in the fate of the Other which falls outside of my responsibility, but also quantitatively infinite because the fate of the entire world rests on my shoulders (*responsable de tout*) (**AE** 147/115). And let us note well: the "absence' of the third person does not in any way excuse me from responsibility for her. I am just as responsible for the distant Other as I am for the one close to me at this moment—just as responsible for the future Others as for those already present (**AE** 204/160). With regard to the guiding theme of this book, this implies that human rights based in the right of the Other person such as Levinas defines it exhibit a universal extension for my responsibility and goodness. As an Other person, each of us has a right to recognition, promotion and assistance.

THE ETHICAL NECESSITY OF A JUST SOCIO-POLITICAL ORDER

How we can realize this heteronomous responsibility for all people? After all, it is easy enough to *say* that I am responsible for everyone, but quite another thing to clarify the necessary conditions for this all-encompassing responsibility to become effectively possible.

SOCIO-ECONOMIC MEDIATION OF UNIVERSAL RESPONSIBILITY

An important dimension of this universal responsibility can be understood as "institutional mediation" (**EFP** 117). What Levinas calls the "third party" includes not just one other Other but very many "absent" thirds, that is to say very many Others whom I can not actually reach but still must try to take into consideration, if only indirectly. This indirect, or non-immediate consideration occurs through the "extension" or "mediation" of all sorts of structures, establishments, organs, and social "objectivations." In this sense, we might speak of a specific sort of "social totality" of subjects in relation to one another neither via a concept nor in the direct *face-à-face* but according to an impersonal and objective field of institutions (**MT** 356/28). Note that the adjective "social" qualifies the word "totality" in a way setting it apart from the very different notion of totality which results from egocentric reduction of the Other(s).

A crucial aspect of this social "mediation" is the "economic." We have already seen how heteronomous responsibility can only be economic: one can not approach the Other with empty hands, but must (and arguably always does) incarnate one's responsibility in a material gift. There is no real "inter-individual economy." On the ground of the universality of responsibility, it must in fact pass immediately into "social economy." This brings us upon economy in the strict sense of the word, i.e. as socially structured and organized care for the Other with the third person as point of departure.

Concretely, it is possible to reach the third economically because I, as a physical, embodied being, bring forth "works" (*oeuvres*), or "products." It is typical of these "works" that the producer—the ego—in one and the same act, or work, both expresses and externalizes himself, and also withdraws. Thus, the work does indeed say something about the one who has produced it, but the two can not be equated. To produce something, in other words, is both to express oneself and to hand that expression, that product, over to its own destiny (**TI** 150-151/175-176). In this way, the work is taken up in a wider field of meaning than can be enclosed within the reign of the ego. And the fact that my work can be manipulated and exchanged permits me to reach the third person: that is to say, precisely through works and not through a word, unless the word is objectivated into a work, as for example a letter, a book, or the registration and commitment of a voice to one or another audio or video system.

Through objectivity, the exchangeability and salability of works can comprise an "economic totality." Here, economy means organization and totalization. Economic interaction brings people together in a specific form of totality in which responsible subjects are maintained in their unicity and yet also taken up into an impersonal objective structure. It is at this juncture that the idea of totality can be said to retain both its power and its positive significance. The economic totality precedes and anticipates the universality of knowledge which surveys and circumscribes everything in a transcendental gaze. Totality is played out first in the arena of mutual dependence between people, especially in the domain of labor and exchange. Thus do people become human totality, or simply humanity (**MT** 366/ 38).

This concrete totality also implies the objectivity of the thing, which further presupposes an agreement about that thing. In the objectivity of the thing I therefore already see the Face of the Other. To think the thing as "objective" means to think it in relation to the Others. Ultimately, the "objective" is that which everyone recognizes. Things are universal—thus not from me, or of me, but from and of everyone, in so far as their being is comprised first as gift, or possibility of gift. In their objectivity, things point to Others, to whom they are given or for whom they can be put to use accommodating their nakedness and need. Through their objectivity, and through the fact that they can be bought and sold, things thus make possible the relation of everyone to everyone. In this sense, economic universality is also concrete universality, or concreteness itself (**SA** 17).

ECONOMIC INTERACTION AND MONEY

In the realization of this concrete, economic totality, an important role is reserved for money. According to Levinas, money fulfills an intermediary function (**TI** 150-151/175-176), or better: as middle term it is the intermediary par excellence. Notwithstanding the variety of functions, roles, and forms it exhibits in the many conjunctures of the economic order—and this includes a prestigious and spectacular, sometimes even monstrous concentration in financial powers and "super-powers," all rendered so photogenic on television—its distinctive and enduring characteristic consists in the fact that it can be exchanged for all manner of things and services (**SA** 14).

Take, to begin with, things, or what we often refer to as "goods." Through the capacity of money to quantify things and set a price on them, their value—precisely as accommodation for human need—becomes calculable. Through the abstract and quantitative-mathematical character of money, things lose their blunt substantiality and become manipulable: one can move them and trade them. Because money is always number, the value of things can be expressed in the amount of their price, which is to say in recognizable and comparable units which, moreover, can be exchanged. In a certain sense, by making things exchangeable, money thus undoes the heterogeneity of each thing with respect to the others. Money makes it possible to buy things and "possess" them, but also to sell them. This means that as possession and property they are at once not at all to be given away and yet at the same time indeed susceptible to sale or trade. Money intercedes in my relation to things in such a way that they are no longer referred solely to my identity (i.e., enclosed within the "identity of the same"), but already opened on to the circuit of exchange. A world which is exchangeable is a world that has lost its heavy materiality simply by allowing itself to be represented by money. The fact that things can be bought and sold means that money is not a possession *in actu* so much as the very possibility and capacity to make something into a possession. Through this possibility which is not itself a possession, the free will of the possessor attains a certain indeterminacy and a degree of life and creativity holding open the possibility of other decisions (**SA** 14).

It is precisely through this potentiality of money, coupled with its abstract and objectively neutral character, that money acquires the institutional function so obvious in our day and age. One knows well how in our industrialized society the use of money has developed into permanent circulation. Money has become a handy and convenient means which stock markets, banks, and all sorts of financial institutions have learned how to render it still more abstract through efficient use of such current technology as appears in checking accounts, credit cards, automatic tellers and electronic payment, all of which threatens to increase its essential anonymity perhaps into infinity... As a means, or instrument, money works not only quickly and easily, but also independently. Money has become virtually equivalent with the transaction of money; one can handle it without ever touching or using it: money without money (**SA** 16).

Naturally, all of these functions of money hold not only for things but also for services, thus not only for the products of labor but also for the labor itself, and not only for acts and achievements but also for the creative ideas and development in and behind them. The commercial relation is also the exchange of good processes (**EFP** 123). Through the existence of money, it is possible for us to buy and sell, to negotiate and trade all manner of labor and services. As means, money introduces a strange and remarkable ambiguity into human society. As potential to buy or borrow services, money does not only plug us immediately into the economic system: at the same time, it also makes it possible for one person to determine and dispose of another—as it were, possessing him. Money, in short, makes it possible to calculate an economic worth for both things *and other people*. A price can be set on a person simply because she offers labor and services for pay. Meanwhile, our technocratic society is presently such that that relation to other people—labor and services for money—is increasingly entrenched and prolific. And the means or form in which money functions as medium of compensation changes not at all the fact that it submits people to calculation and estimation. As "price," this calculus is everywhere, including the plane of the interpersonal. In the economic order, a human being is seen not only as one who gives, receives, produces, buys and sells goods, but also one who can be bought, traded or sold precisely on the basis of his or her production capacity, understood as expertise and "know-how" the economic worth of which can be expressed in terms of capital. In this sense, the human being becomes a commodity. Already in Marx, we are directed to the idea that wages are in no sense a reward. Wages represent the means by which a person is bought. This implies objectivization and integration, as a "function" of the economic totality. Obviously, this is a scandal, and yet it also presents itself as the danger to be taken for the promise of necessary liberty and freedom of movement within the system. Through the fact that there is a price on her labor and services, and that she herself can set a price on them (within the limits of what the market allows), she remains to a certain extent able define and determine herself, notwithstanding the fact that she remains only a part of the economy which she must engage from her separateness (SA 16).

Money not only makes goods and services exceptionally accessible, thus drawing both people and things into a single economic order, but it also makes them increasingly alike, so that what distinguishes them, locating them, as it were, on a different level becomes much less clear. Though all goods depend on human labor, things and services nonetheless represent two heterogeneous orders. But when they are expressed in terms of money or currency, or in terms of the respective prices set on them, they become immediately comparable, so that their difference is levelled-down or even erased, hence arriving in an equalizing totality. The homogeneity which this implies is strictly paradoxical. The reduction of labor and services to their objective worth, expressed as either need or financial amount, thus submitting goods and services to a single denominator, clouds our view of the incalculable value of labor as a typically human activity therefore to be "measured" according to principles very different than that of calculation and exchange. Thanks to the fact of wages, labor and human services are associated with goods and objectified, so that the labor itself—which, after all, does lie behind all goods—is forgotten. One appropriates labor and service buy buying and selling: essential moment in a culture of money such as we inhabit (SA 16). This scandal becomes greater still when, as Marx has shown, a concrete economic system (capitalism) even assigns a "surplus value" to material goods—including labor. Nonetheless, the calculation and quantitative measurement introduced everywhere by money and exchange—the very origin of money—does liberate us from the difficulties, surprises, and subjective aspirations at work in simple bartering.

Yet, in this way, via money, goods and labor or things and services do come to form an objective whole, an economic totality, in which people can quickly, easily, and efficiently reach one another, even if this also means that they are only "thirds" to one another. Together with "economic work," money makes possible a real society in which each of us can take up his or her responsibility for the others without always meeting them directly (**MT** 372-373/44-45). This economic totality, thus making possible our universal responsibility, is of a very specific nature. It is not of the type which, obeying a formal or logical structure of parts and wholes, swallows each part into the whole without leaving behind a trace. The totality of the economic order is a whole in which those who, as buyers, determine the use of our own money become commodities ourselves, but without losing all breathing space or giving up our souls in the process. In this way, both money and the organization of financial traffic and exchange can contribute in their own way to the formation of a socio-economic totality by which people can enter into interaction and form a whole without that whole erasing or qualifying their separateness and individuality (**SA** 17).

Finally, it is also important to notice how the essential structure of money, in its function as mediator and means to interaction, always presupposes the *face-à-face*. Notwithstanding the fact that money seems to function on the level of satisfaction of needs and thus, more deeply, the level of self-interest, in its capacity to provide an ever-improving mode of exchange of goods and services between people, it also expresses the original situation of the I-Other relation. Exchange, buying and selling, payment and repayment: these are not possible unless people enter into relations with one another, with each thus binding herself to the other. As meeting or encounter, economic exchange is neither a pure union of one individual with another, nor a violent conquest of one by another, nor, of course, simply the perception of an object that offers itself in its truth, but an attachment to one another defined essentially by the responsibility embodied in apportionment and sharing. When using money, one must therefore always bear in mind the interhuman dimension of proximity—the sociality of unique individual with and to unique individual, literally, the "trans-action" from which all money flows and which always animates and re-animates it (**SA** 14).

NECESSITY OF A SOCIAL "ORDER"

The need for, and possibility of institutional, socio-economic means for our universal responsibility is still not the last word on this matter. The affirmation of the all-encompassing scope of one's responsibility-to-and-for-the-Other brings us immediately to the problem of ordering the means to live it in society. Were there only two of us in the world, I and the Other, this question would never arise. That one Other person would fall completely and unmistakably under my responsibility. In paradise, one can speak of an unlimited love between Adam and Eve, because they were there together alone, but in the real world, there are of course many Others, both near and far, intimate and functional, present and absent, now and future, all in relation with one another the most differing but also intersecting ways: "the third party is other than the neighbor, but also another neighbor, and also a neighbor of the other, and not simply his equal." (AE 200/157) In this sense, I can never do complete justice to my relation to the Other with "his Other," not even were it so that I am responsible for the Other alone. This one person standing before me and for whom I am responsible can not free himself of his responsibility for other Others. Likewise, those other Others—those "third parties"—also have their own responsibilities which lie beyond the field of my vision but which nonetheless touch me (ND 57).

So long as responsibility moves from the ego to only one Other, it has a purely rectilinear and unitary meaning. But immediately upon the entrance of the third, there arises the question "Who is most my neighbor? Who comes first, my neighbor or the third?" Through the fact that the Other is in relation with thirds, I can injure or deprive those thirds by taking up my responsibility for that Other—even if I discharge it fully and correctly. I can also carry out a particular economic service for a third, but very possibly at the price—and without my intending it—of negative consequences for other thirds for whom I am also responsible. Hence Levinas' paradoxical statement that "The Other and the third, my neighbors, contemporaries of one another, put distance between me and the other party" (AE 200/157). To the degree that I effectively achieve my responsibility for the third, I also do injustice to my neighbor. If I direct my attention to my neighbor, I am doubtless negligent toward the thirds who are beyond the radius of my activity, thus victimized by oversight. In the background of all of this, there lurks the penetrating and dramatic clarity of biblical rhetoric: "Peace, peace to the neighbor and the one far-off" (*Isaiah* 57:19; **AE** 200/157). I must bring peace to both the neighbor and the one far off, and precisely therein lies the great difficulty of the good life. The third introduces a tension, or even a contradiction in the pure and lofty responsibility of being "one-for-the-Other." The third places limits on my infinite responsibility for the one Other person who faces me. The hunger of the Other, we have seen, is an absolute demand which permits no exception, no qualification and no calculation, but orders an immediate and total commitment of my resources. And yet there is my responsibility for those other Others. "Only the hunger of the third," writes Levinas, "limits the rights of the Other" (**DL** 12/XIV). The limitation involved here is, of course, completely different than the "limitation of animality," of the ego's selfish totalization as it strives toward self-justification and self-determination. There is certainly no question here of the basic ethical orientation of an ego responsibility to the Other and for the Other. Rather, it is a matter of factual, relative limitations in the potential response to the one Other who faces the ego, as imposed by a necessity to take account of all Others at once.

This "tension" in responsibility itself implicates the ego in "comparing the incomparable" (**PP** 345/167-168), that is to say it requires the ego to bring the incomparable goodness encountered in the unique Other into balance with the rights of all Others who are equally unique (**U** 306). The universality of my responsibility requires me to compare the unique Other with all Others, to exercise my powers of calculation and generalization. The guarantee of this responsibility for Others near and far, today and tomorrow, transgresses my responsibility and goodness for the one Other here and now. I must take account of everyone. I must confront and judge, weigh and balance, rank, distinguish, and measure, rule and control, in short "moderate" (**DHDA** 183). The situation of concrete inter-human engagements and responsibilities must be "surveyed and estimated." From this analysis, there must then emerge an evaluation of the situation. In other words, priorities must be established (**AE** 201/158). Above all, I must devise a plan which stipulates the progress or sequence of my actions and their approach. I must therefore conduct myself to the Others, and sit with them at the table, clarifying appointments and agreements meant to reduce the many possible contradictions, obstructions, and interferences opposing or complicating the exercise of my different responsibilities, so as to insure as much balance as possible. In short, we can not effectively achieve this unlimited responsibility to and for one another unless we enter into discussion and agreement (**HAH** 107/133 note 11).

THE SOCIAL NECESSITY OF
KNOWLEDGE, SCIENCE, AND LANGUAGE

Such agreement presupposes conscious reflection. In order to really take up our universal responsibility, we must first thematize and then actively engage the concrete field of our different engagements, both inter-human and institutional. This implies the necessity of representation and objectivating thought, and in turn "theory." From the moment that we are with three, there emerges a need to critically reflect and understand. This formation of theory is incarnated and further elaborated in philosophy and the sciences (**DVI** 132/82).

Of course, reflective thematization is impossible without verbalization. With the third, there also emerges objective mediation via the system of language: "were there only two of us on earth, there would be no words: one would not speak. Objective language begins only when there are three" (**ND** 57). Reflection on the coordination and ordering of responsibilities can take place concretely only through the means of a verbal communication no longer simply "communication of communication itself" (as with the face), but involves the objective announcement of messages and content. In order for this communication to proceed as smoothly as possible, one makes spontaneous recourse to written language: to objective reports, contracts, and contracts, reference books and "writings" (books, letters, pamphlets, articles, etc.), all of which Levinas characterizes together as "the Said" (*le Dit*; **AE** 78/62).

It is clear that this part of Levinas' analysis aims at revalorizing the negative evaluation placed on noetic totalization, now to be con-

ceived as means of social ordering or organization in line with responsibility-to-and-for-the-Other. He thus also takes the view that
those of us who carry on that noetic and verbal totalization flirt with
nihilism, for the latter denies not only the worth of consciousness,
thought, philosophy, and science, but also the very responsibility
which require them to take shape and be achieved. Nonetheless, it is
also necessary to constantly unmask, or "Unsay" (*dédit*), the objective Said of reflection, comparison, judgment, coordination and agreement, since the moment in which they make possible the achievement of universal responsibility is also a moment of betrayal, of con-
finement of the pre-original "Saying" (*le Dire*), one-to-the-Other,
back into the totality of the Said. Furthermore, this ambiguous moment, in which the first word of responsibility, the "Here I am" which
expresses the ego's responsibility-to-the-Other-and-for-the-Other, is
simultaneously the moment of responsibility for the other Others.
The "Here I am" is at once a response to my neighbor and an open-
ing on to responsibility for all. In my responsibility as "one-for-the-
Other," it is also necessary to take account of the rights all third
parties.

According to Levinas, it is precisely here that one finds all of the
riches of Athens, with its love of wisdom, knowledge, and understanding. However, this love of wisdom, this philos-sophia, does not
come first, but only after or in light of the rather different riches of
Jerusalem, with its wisdom of love, with the "priority of the Other as
command" (in the Torah) grounding all thinking and theory. While
Greek wisdom therefore does not have priority, and even depends on
biblical wisdom in order to achieve its truth and justice, still, says
Levinas, it is indispensable for us (**EFP** 117). To the degree that it,
too, is inspired by "extravagant love of the Other," it shares in the
wisdom of love—or better, it becomes the wisdom of love, in the
strict sense of the word (**U** 306). Regarding content, it is not only the
Greek heritage which stands in need of the biblical tradition, but
also biblical wisdom which needs Greek wisdom (**PP** 345/168).

JUSTICE IN THE STRICT SENSE

In this word, there must be not only love of neighbor (*charité*), but also justice (**AE** 204/160). In the context of the presence of the third, the concept of justice receives a stricter clarification than it has in the context of the direct I-Other relation, as Levinas himself admits: "The word 'justice' is in effect much more in its place, there, where equity is necessary and not my 'subordination' to the Other. If equity is necessary, there must also be comparison and equality: equality between those that cannot be compared. And consequently, the word 'justice' applies much more to the relationship with the third party than to the relationship with the Other" (**DVI** 132/82). In the period of *Totalité et Infini*, Levinas uses the word justice as a synonym for the ethical, for responsibility, for the rights of the Other in the broad sense (**PM** 171). In his introduction to the German translation of that work (1987), Levinas explicitly states that it is better to clearly distinguish between love of neighbor, or mercy, and justice, which is a matter of the third and the implied need for reflection and arrival at some sort of balance. At the same time, he repeats that there is a close and forceful connection between these two. This is expressed unmistakably in the universality of the face, which points in its essential structure toward all others. The face, Levinas has said, is the face of faces (*le visage des visages*; **AE** 204/160). Hence is responsibility for the thirds, understood as justice in the strict sense of the word, a direct extension of "original sociality" (**U** 306), of the creatural responsibility-to-and-for-the-Other, understood as justice in the broad and embracing sense (**DVI** 135-136/84-86). In order to avoid confusing the two, we might therefore reserve for the domain of the third the expression "social justice." The third, Levinas has said, is the beginning of a relative and distributed justice. It is her entrance on the scene which makes necessary a "just co-existence" which regulates and structures, or perhaps better, orders a reasonable—a rationally mediated—equality and equanimity (**ND** 58). From this it follows immediately that I can not restrict my original responsibility for the Other solely to the alleviation of concrete need *hic et nunc*. To the contrary, the universal and all-encompassing character of my responsibility requires me to also take account of the structural context in which this need presents itself. It is possible that, in the long run, I can really do something for the Other only if I enter into the "system" in which her need presents itself or which in fact causes it. Charity must become structural justice if its ethical nature is to become truly effective.

Justice in the strict sense, however, means a continual correction and limitation of the ethical asymmetry between me and the Other. I, too, am an Other for the Other and for the third. The original inequality of my infinite responsibility for the unique Other is corrected in this sense of the word through the fact that I, too, fall under the responsibility of Others. Through the presence of a third, I am an Other like the Others, that is to say, their equal. Or better, we are fellows to one another. We stand equally before one another. It is as if we appear together only before a tribunal which judges us equally. With the appearance of the third, symmetry enters proximity, but without abolishing the difference, the ethical non-indifference. Equality constitutes our co-presence: we are "together-in-one-place," "as one" and without hierarchy. This makes reciprocity possible; equality must now be situated on the level of "social structure." The fact that we are on equal footing with one another means that the face of the Other is undone from its transcendence and always withdrawing "invisibility." It is instead presented as a theme, or rather re-presented, situated in the order of the now, the present (**AE** 163/127). We become objectively accessible to one another; we fall under one another's objectivating intentionality. Synchronized co-existence undoes the Face of its Face-ness (**PP** 345/168): "*le Visage se dé-visage*" (**AE** 201/158). Concretely, this consists in withdrawing from the Other her irreducibility and incomparable unicity, defining her instead by her individuality, which can be considered as a single instance of a wider genre, hence comparable, susceptible to measurement and objectivation. While the Other is and remains unique, she is also, precisely as a third, part of a general type or sort (**AS** 61). The Other as unique is pre-logical, not of "wild thinking" (Lévi-Straus), but that which escapes and evens precedes all thinking. But the third signifies the return of the logical, that is to say of conceptualizing, comparing, categorizing, apportioning, and ordering, in short generalizing (**EFP** 117).

There is more. For one to belong to the syncronicity or simultaneity of the social structure is also to have one's autonomy restored. We are all assembled in an order according to which each "in himself" counts just as much as any Other, and as a self-standing ego, regardless of the fact of other persons. Or so, at least, it should be. Through the social order introduced by the third, subjectivity is once again revealed to be an ego, as contemporaneity, a "beginning" and "principle," an "act of intelligence and freedom." This revaluation of the ego is in no sense that restorative proclamation of subjectivity voiced by Fichte, for whom the subject is its own adequate origin. In contrast, Levinas' path to the "ego" departs not from autonomy but instead the ethical "self": the accusative is the source of the nominative. The autonomous and self-identifying ego belongs to the level of social order which, via the third, is derived from universal responsibility (**AE** 207-208/162-164). It is on the ground of this social identity that there can be justice and equality for both I and the Other, thus for everyone. Even I myself am subject to such calculation and comparison. And "fortunately," we might add. Were there only my responsibility for the unique Other, everything would depend on me: *personne ne peut se substituer à moi tant que moi*—no one can be substituted for me in so far as me (**DVI** 135/84). My responsibility is total and inalienable. But, "thanks to God," I am not alone: there are Others who also have their own responsibility, as radical as mine. "Fortunately," I too fall under the responsibility of Others both near and far (**AE** 202/159). Hence is there a communal space of identity and reciprocity (**EFP** 123) in which I and the Others all partake, in which I and the Others are counted together, and where, as a citizen, I have as many common, ordered rights and duties as does anyone else. And what insures that these rights and duties come to a just and equitable balance is precisely the natural and evident competition between duties and between rights (**AE** 204/160). On the level of the unique Other, I am uniquely responsible, but on the level of the third I am also an Other for the Other: the original and fundamental asymmetry becomes a derived symmetry (**AS** 72). This also marks the reemergence of human rights and the right to freedom. They are no longer the expression of merciless self-interest, but the realization of reciprocal recognition of one another's equality and autonomy as deserving respect.

The Ethical Necessity of a
Just Politics in World Perspective

Such a social justice can come truly into being only through a whole array of establishments, structures, and agencies. Social responsibility must be legislated by institutional and structural means (**AE** 163/ 127). Juridical, familial, economic, and social units require a degree of regulation from the state, coordinated and represented by an "informed and impartial authority" (**SA** 19): "the metaphysics of the relation with the Other is achieved in service and hospitality. In the measure that the face of someone else truly brings us into relation with the third, the metaphysical relation from me to the Other takes the form of a we, and flows into a state, institutions and laws, which form the source of universality" (**TI** 276/299-300). Though the ethics of responsibility, as primary experience, might at first sight seem to eschew politics and the state, in fact due to the complexity of a plural reality it is inextricably and essentially interwoven with them. Politics and the state might be said to rest on an insufficiency of love of neighbor, which must go beyond itself if indeed it is to establish and fulfill itself for the many in a plural space and time (**AEG** 33).

However, the state is not yet the last word in Levinas' treatment of "communal life." He urges us beyond the state to a still more universal—a truly universal—society encompassing all of humanity. The establishment of a state means, in fact, the creation of a socio-political structure which for the most part rests on a "people" or "nation," or is at least the structured assembly of a particular group of people. In such a group, socio-political order is always partly determined by ethnic or national interests, even if only through resistance and conflict. If, however, universal responsibility were to be incarnated only in states or nations, it would fall far short of its call to serve all people. The limitations imposed by the relative particularity of the nation in which responsibility is always enacted therefore threaten that responsibility with what we might think of as "national egoism," with a return of individual egoism now on the national scale. What then results—to speak by way of analogy with the inter-individual one against all—is irreducible conflict between each nation and all the others. Western civilization has long known the certain consequences: struggle for hegemony, with all of the accompanying alliances contributing to antagonism of still greater proportions, a lust for international conquest, and colonialism of every sort, whether direct or indirect (**LPI** 50). According to Levinas, national egoism characterizes the pagan state, the "state of Caesar" jealously guarding its sovereignty: "the state in search of hegemony; the conquering, imperialist, totalitarian, and oppressive state" (**AV** 216/184). But the universality of responsibility makes the principle of sovereign inviolability as such and as "endpoint" simply indefensible. Yet without that responsibility, states (or even united states) always threaten to pervert their own claim on sovereignty, driving toward an international egoism from which there can be expected nothing but a "struggle for life and death," with all of the incumbent arms races and convulsive efforts to widen spheres of influence. National (and egocentric) sovereignty thus hinders each nation's responsibility to the other nations, but above all to the "poor, widowed, and orphaned" suffering under each of them. And this, Levinas has shown, flows directly from responsibility-to-and-for-the-Other.

Hence must "national justice" be transcended in favor of a "universal justice" (**QLT** 141-142/66). The final aim of universal responsibility is a worldwide community in which all people are equal and no one is excluded or suppressed by others. This human society with a global dimension, coextensive with humanity itself, but built on an accord consisting neither in contracts forged nor wars survived, Levinas calls the creatural solidarity of ethical fraternity in being "one-for-the-Other." "Only the idea of humanity makes justice, even national justice, possible insofar as [justice must be] unconditional and irrevocable. The idea of humanity counterbalances the threat of war weighing on every purely national [form of] justice" (**LPI** 51). In designating this universal society based on ethical fraternity, Levinas turns to his Jewish background, speaking of "messianic politics." This would seem to fall at least partly in line with a political interpretation of messianism present in Judaism alongside the prophetic and priestly interpretations. The Messiah is then seen as a prince from the House of David, with the task of freeing the people of Israel and founding a just society characterized by peace, or "shalom." Only when there is inter-human peace as well as political peace can God come, announcing the future, or eschatological world (**AV** 213/181, 217-218/185-186). Against this background, Levinas envisions a supra-national, global human society characterized by a peace which is "messianic" (**TI** x/22). Peace is truly peace only if national and international particularism is transcended, freeing us to live by universal responsibility (**AE** 20/17). This peace, finally, no longer merely results from the suppression or avoidance of war, but flows from the unconditional, non-indifference of fraternal solidarity (**LPI** 49, 52).

CHAPTER 5
AN ALWAYS BETTER JUSTICE AND THE "SMALL GOODNESS"

A Marxist might think that with the affirmation of a necessity for socio-political order everything has been said. Nothing could be less true. Coming from his experience of the Holocaust, Levinas is extremely apprehensive at the suggestion that politics and the State would have the last word in our human relations.

THE FACE-À-FACE AS PERMANENT SOURCE OF

EVERY SOCIO-POLITICAL ORDER

To begin with, according to Levinas it is of the greatest importance not only to affirm the necessity of the State, as well as of going beyond it to a universal society with rights, laws, structures, and institutions, but also, and still more, to call them back repeatedly to their ethical origin and basis. In order to be humane or ethical, each socio-political order must build on the unlimited responsibility of each ego for every Other: "my relation with the Other as my neighbor gives meaning to my relations with all Others. All human relations as human proceed from disinterestedness" (**AE** 202/159). The one-for-the-Other of solidarity and proximity is not a misformed abstraction but, to the contrary, justice in *stricto sensu*: the justice allegedly detached from responsibility would be an abstraction. "It is evident that the possession of universal laws is the best way to protect the neighbor. Justice is necessary, but is in the final account motivated by the face of the Other" (**WZE** 148). Social justice is meaningful only because—or if—it builds on "significance par excellence," the

proximity of ethical fraternity or responsible solidarity. Nothing—
neither politics, law, the State, institutions and society, nor labor,
technology, money, business and all other forms of "exchange"—can
exempt itself from responsibility one-for-the-Other. Civil justice and
the law are not at all a degradation or deformation of the "one for the
Other," not at all a reduction, limitation or even neutralization of
anarchic responsibility, not at all a degeneration appearing the moment the initial "two" becomes a factual "three" or "many" (**EI** 86/
80). "Justice (in the strict sense) remains justice only in a society
where there are no distinctions between those who are near and those
who are far off, but where it remains impossible to pass by the clos-
est. The equality of all is borne by my inequality, by the preponder-
ance of my duty over my rights. The forgetting of oneself moves
justice" (**AE** 203/159). This makes it exceptionally clear how for Levinas the inter-personal relation serves as the basic norm for a society
of many. In contrast with Hobbes' political philosophy, which bases
society on the need to set limits on human passion, on our bestiality,
the political philosophy of Levinas builds unambiguously on the claim
that we are each "created" first and wholly for the Other. Since we are
many, we must set limits on our original or creatural goodness, and
take up the wisdom of love, that is to say a reflective justice of love.
Justice consists in a delimitation of love of neighbor, not delimitation of mutual animosity. In this sense, love and justice are inseparable and simultaneous, unless one finds oneself marooned on an
island without a third person. Love of neighbor is impossible without justice, and without love of neighbor justice degenerates into
violence (**WZE** 150).

In this connection, Levinas points to the need for a "prophetic"
word such as was recognized and found in Israel, where the prophet
voiced his bold and challenging words not only to particular people
but also the king himself, which is to say to the State. The prophet's
work was neither clandestine nor aimed at revolution. What is remarkable is that in the Bible the king immediately accepts this interrogation: "C'est un drôle de roi!"—*strange king, that one!* In contrast
with the false prophets and prophet guilds who flatter and toady to
the king, the true prophet points an uncompromising an unflinch-
ing finger at both the people and the king, awakening them to the

"ethical." This does not mean that the Jewish Scriptures condemn the State as such, but that they protest against a pure assimilation of the State with "world politics" and the egocentric-totalizing laws of the *do ut des*, with all of the accompanying power conflicts, intrigues, strategies, battles, and balancing acts. What angered the prophet Samuel when he was asked for a king was not the request itself but the fact that what was wanted was a king specifically "like all the other nations have." In line with the doctrine on royal power recorded in *Deuteronomy*, Samuel can not accept a king as such—as final norm of principle—but only a State that stands under the Law (*Torah*): a socio-political order which is normativized ethically. According to Levinas, the idea of an ethical State is thus a biblical idea.

The "affliction" of justice, which rests on unlimited asymmetrical responsibility, must therefore be the "spirit" of social life. This means that those who design, operate, and maintain our social structures and institutions must themselves be "possessed" by the ethical responsibility of "one-for-the-Other." Structures and laws can function ethically only when in the hands of people of (ethical) good will. We might also think of this as a plea for "saints" in politics. For Levinas, the "saintliness" of the one who acts for a solidarity resting on responsibility for the Other is the foundation not only of ethics, but also politics: the just State will flow from justice and saintliness, rather than from propaganda and predication. In other words, justice is not an automatic consequence of institutions. These are only instances of objectivization, or "mediation," and must be repeatedly "inspired" and "animated" anew. Justice is impossible unless the one who is to achieve it finds herself within responsibility to and for the Other. Its function can not be limited to passing judgment, or subsuming particular cases under a general rule. The judge is not to be found outside of the conflict; he is not a spectator but, as an "ego established in responsibility," is always involved and implicated, so the speak, from head to toe. He does not stand outside the game, like a field referee or line judge, but is himself one of the players. In short, he is truly a judge only if and when he judges—lives his judgeship—from a radical ethical responsibility for the accused. Of course, as with any exercise of freedom and responsibility, this single relation with the accused can not and must not separated or abstracted from his relations with injured third parties or victims, for whom the judge, *via his responsibility for the accused*, is also responsible. In this sense, responsibility in the second person must be the heart of the law, that is to say the heart of responsibility in the third person. The equanimity and comparative equality of justice must be indicated and authorized, guided and moved, by the ethical meaning and orientation of the "one for the Other" (**AE** 116/91-92, 204/160). A concrete illustration of this argument can be found in a short commentary Levinas wrote on the occasion of a visit by Soviet premier Khruschev to France, in 1960: "In a system where all that counts are the principles of an impersonal Discourse, this trip confirms, against every such system, the necessity of personal good will and moral intention, of a coexistence without system. It points, beyond the universal structure, to the importance of relations individual to individual, of person to person, thus of the need to see behind anonymous principles to the face of the other person" (**DL** [1963] 223-224). Individual ethical responsibility for the Other is completely indispensable. In this connection, Levinas also refers to his vision as "ethical individualism" (**TH** 103/22-23).

The Need for an Always Improving
Justice and Freedom

The individual responsibility of being one-for-the-Other is not only the constant source of nourishment for socio-political order, but also functions as its constant corrective, and in different ways.

No Definitive Regime

This holds true above all with regard to the formation and realization of socio-political justice itself. Justice in its concrete realization never suffices. It has constant need of review, reform, and improvement. It also does not suffice that the socio-political structures are "possessed" by the *face-à-face*. Alone, this would leave them undisturbed, unmoved to constant reform. It is necessary for them to always submit themselves to new critique in order to remain certain that they still answer to the ethical and just intentions at their origin.

For their anonymous façade makes it virtually inevitable that responsible subjects will, from time to time, find it difficult to recognize the concern with peace and justice which properly guides them. It is for precisely this reason that all socio-political functions and institutions must be submitted to repeated interrogation as to whether they respond sufficiently to their own unconditionally ethical meaning— that is to say, whether or to what degree they are indeed the structural realization of justice and peace for everyone, both near and far, present and future (**I** 130-131/243-244).

We might illustrate this need for constant vigilance and critique in the economic domain: because of the existence of the third, the State can and must require us to give, meaning to pay taxes and contribute to all sorts of programs of solidarity. Note well, however, that this means that taxes and financial contributions are no longer motivated by a self-interestedness forced to compromise, but instead a mercy and compassion which can and must translate into economic justice. *In concreto*, taxes are a form of giving; one gives to a society that collects money and apportions it. This is completely legitimate. There is the law, and our entire lives have a legal character. However, imbalance and injustice do remain possible at this level. There is such a thing as overly equal distribution of taxes, as for instance when they are excessive, no longer calculated or, more literally, no longer balanced or proportionate. In this sense, economic organization must always be subject to discussion with a constant eye to the improvement or renewal of justice. Moreover, this holds not only for economics, but also in the social, juridical, legal, and political domains. We have an ongoing need for an ever-improved and improving legal and juridical structures, social organization, and political order (**SA** 19).

This implies that socio-political justice and peace in their present forms must never become a definitive regime and this against our western political thinking, with its pretension to universality, and lack of patience for the struggle to improve, exhibiting instead the contrary tendency toward installing itself as an absolute and unchanging system located outside of time (**AS** 62). Indeed, every economic, juridical, social, and political system exhibits this same irresistible tendency toward presenting itself as the *Ein und Alles*. In this sense, it is totalitarian in intention, and sometimes even in the hard reality of its apparatus. Think, for example, of the economic totality, realized by, among other things, money: the inevitable manifestation of the separateness of each participant naturally calls up anxiety at the possibility of totalization, above all when one leaves the system to itself, so that it quickly becomes all-powerful. This anxiety with respect to one or another totalization—socio-political or economic—is at bottom the return of horror at the "there is" (*il y a*). And indeed, every totalitarianism displays a deep affinity with the "there is," precisely where it de-personalizes each unique person into a "no-thing" or "no-one" (**SA** 17).

The charity of "one-for-the-Other" is never completely fulfilled by public justice or any socio-political system. This is why there is always a need for better justice and greater peace, indeed sometimes even a new justice and a new peace—*ad infinitum*. According to Levinas, the fact that public justice is never complete should prevent it from the temptation of solidifying into a definitive regime capable of exercising, as it were, the last word, and of passing conclusive judgment on every situation. An example of the latter is the totalitarian planned economies, notwithstanding the claim that they are erected and enforced in the name of justice and peace. As Levinas sees it, this is precisely what happened in Stalinist Russia (**AS** 62) which, as a totalitarian regime, stood directly in the way of constant renewal of justice and peace. Moreover, this was not merely an accidental property of historical Stalinism. To seek a society in which love of neighbor is fully and immediately realized, in other words to capture love of neighbor in a single, organized system, is to run the risk of Stalinism (**EFP** 97-98). One forgets that justice and peace must be perpetually reborn out of responsibility and goodness. In this connection, Levinas also makes the provocative remark that there is indeed love of neighbor in Marxism, but that after Stalinism it is no longer permissible to speak of Marxism. There are three moments in a totalitarian regime: the violence of rigidity, reduction to a single end, and administration. Together, they form a "system" which considers Stalinism the ultimate incarnation of justice.

Opposed to this is the non-totalitarian, or so-called "liberal" regime in which society is called repeatedly to recognize the inadequacy of each successive incarnation of peace and justice, and in turn driven to renew it. This implies a constant need for critical vigilance over the political institution and its leaders, for they are never just or peaceful enough. It is to this end that we, in our democratic society, recognize the freedom of the press and freedom of speech on matters of conscience and individual responsibility (**DHDA** 185). In this respect, the future may be said to consist in the openness which flows from our constant lag behind justice and the demands of charity (**AS** 92-93). This "coming too late" is perceived by the responsible and free ego, which never accords completely with the system or with organized justice, and therefore—whether as poet, singer, innocent child, simple soul, dreamer, or journalist—always can and must submit that system to critique.

Necessity of a "Permanent Revolution"

This demand for an ever better justice also leads Levinas to speak of the need for a "permanent revolution" (**I** 131/243-244).

In order to clarify the precise meaning and scope of this statement, we must take up Levinas' particular understanding of the fashionable word "revolution." According to his ethical perspective, he of course rejects the purely formal sense of the term—as violence, or simple destruction of the existing order. He is even less satisfied with the idea of revolution as "spirit of sacrifice," which is often operative without one realizing it. Under Hitler, there were many who committed to the notion of "trust for trust alone," "submit to submit," or "sacrifice for the sake of sacrifice." With this lesson in mind, Levinas takes the view that revolution must be defined and judged for its content, for the values that it pursues. For Levinas, there can truly be talk of revolution only where people are liberated from the oppression of economic alienation and socio-political determinism. It is thus not enough to be *against* something; one must also be *for* something. One must be in the service of an end, an aim. Or better, one must be in the service of an end or aim which is just, for not all are ethically responsible. Not all are inspired by the responsibility of one-for-the-Other (**DL** 197-198/149-150).

Revolutionary action in the truest sense is thus not to be found in the massive and imposing character of irresistible and aggressive street marches. Fascism, for example, has had enormous success with this sort of action, and yet it would be difficult today to call that a "true" revolution. According to Levinas, revolutionary action is primarily the action of a "solitary" or separated person who prepares the revolution with a torn and troubled conscience, that is to say in the doubly clandestine situation of the catacombs and ethical interiority. It occurs in an extreme conflict of conscience which risks making the revolution itself impossible. And this is a matter not only of avoiding the possibility of handing things over to criminal leaders but also fear of causing the innocent to suffer. In other words, the true revolution can never be detached from *universal* responsibility, from the struggle for justice and liberation for all (**SaS** 38-39/116-117).

This ethical reflection underlying true revolution also furnishes the background necessary for a sketch of what Levinas means by "permanent revolution." He situates his view of this matter within reflections on the many contemporary revolts against the established economic and socio-political order, as for instance Paris saw in May of 1968. These movements are not important because they resist an established "order," but rather because they claim to be *ethical*. They resist a society said to be "without justice" or, more precisely, they resist an existing socio-political order because its injustices are hidden in the form (or appearance) of a socio-political and economic balance governed by objective laws which are themselves subject to a regime of power. This applies regardless of the specific political form in which that power is exercised: whether, on one hand, cities, states, nations, united nations, or on the other hand, labor unions, interest groups, or syndicates whose power sometimes enables them to become veritable "states within the state." The movements revolting against these established powers deserve our attention because their ethical inspiration leads them to seek an "other" or "new"—more just—society. Based on this ethical intention, their voices can become like a clarion call, awakening the citizens of an established order from their dogmatic slumber, confronting them with the degree to which they go along with that order precisely because it serves and protects their own self-interests. In this way, they show concretely how the radical ethical responsibility of the one for the Other, up to and including universal solidarity and justice, must be the "revolutionary dynamite" under all fixed socio-political structures (I 130/242).

This does not yet clearly explain why the revolution must be "permanent." At this point, however, Levinas calls attention to a constant danger threatening every revolution from inside. A revolution which overturns the established order because it was found unjust is itself, as soon as it succeeds, thus coming to power, in danger of taking the same unjust position, as for instance when it presents itself as the final solution. Hence must revolution, or better, "ethical revision," begin again the very moment a new society is installed: "revolt against injustice, which begins the moment that an order is instituted" (I 130/242). As soon as institutions appear in order to protect the new justice, the fruit of the new revolution, they are already, as it were, rigid and senile. In revolution itself there emerges the need for a new and permanent revision, in the form of critique of the new, post-revolutionary, political order—an order which, precisely as "order," will display a tendency to ignore or resist critique, to minimalize it or even suppress it. It is in this sense that Levinas urges a revolution which remains in revolution. Notwithstanding its focus on politics, social and economic doctrine, and "revolutionary technique," it must always strive ultimately to liberate the human person. It must always be and remain what it is in essence, namely dis-order, or "an-archy," breaking through all possible frameworks and horizons. It retains its ethical inspiration only if it remains in a permanent state of the critical resistance to, and revision of socio-political order—a permanent state, in other words, of that which brought it to life in the first place.

In this sense, "permanent revolution" is simply another name for the struggle toward a justice which is never justice enough, thus for a *always improving justice*. In themselves, apart from their deeper ethical inspiration, the established socio-political structures and gestalts might never function. In its "infinity," the ethical selflessness of the "one-for-the-Other" must be the permanent time-bomb under every form of society and politics, insofar as they tend easily to lose sight of their own injustices, missing the difference between "complete justice" and the "half-justices" which are more easily promoted. Ethics must be the permanent purification of the ideology lurking within every socio-political order, as it promotes itself as the sufficient and definitive embodiment of economic, social, and political injustice. It must resist every socio-political conservatism which stubbornly—literally, "with man and power"—attempts to maintain its central position, striving to erase or forget the provisional character of its own mandate by appeal to every manner of "strategies of justice." The ethical ideal of radical selflessness "to and for the Other" must put on trial every form of ideology present in a society, whether manifest or hidden, thus holding open the way toward an always improving justice (**I** 131/243).

JUSTICE WHICH TAKES ACCOUNT OF EVIL

There is another manner in which the need for an always improving justice appears in the socio-political domain.

The accent which we just placed on the ethical necessity of socio-political justice and peace shows that a concern with egocentric forms of so-called justice is by no means uncalled for. There is a real possibility for us to conceive of socio-political justice and peace as the necessary extension of inter-human justice and peace. This leads to the question of the socio-political status of the juridical, as the site of judgment as to what is just and unjust (**AS** 60).

To begin with, it is simply realistic to observe that an ethically committed subject can easily fall back into egocentric, and therefore aggressive, violent behavior. The initially unlimited responsibility-from-and-for-the-Other, called by the interference of the third person to accept limits and make comparisons, can slip into the background where it is quickly lost. Where the necessity of a socio-political justice reinvests the (relative but nonetheless real) autonomy of the ego with a positive value, that ego will immediately try to place its own interests, or more deeply, its innate self-centeredness in the forefront, to the detriment, of course, of the ethical affection of a "being-responsible-for the Other" (**QLT** 108/49, 163/74). In other words, order, totality, the State, politics, science, labor, and technology all have a constant tendency to break from the "for the Other" in

favor of their own power and orientation. In this oblivion of responsibility, egoism returns. And even if it is neither primary (original)
nor ultimate (definitive), still it is really possible. The "one-for-the-
Other" is in permanent danger of slumber or desertion, not only
because it is a heavy assignment but also it must be worked out in the
company of third persons, which requires the (temporary) construction of forms and structures supporting a distance which is no longer
directly focussed on its ethical origin (**AE** 165/128-129, 203/159-
160). The pursuit of socio-political justice will therefore also involve
a struggle against a narcissism which always tries—as the easiest and
broadest path—to refer everything back to the ego, to oneself. Justice is always situated in the ambiguous tension between the attempt
to serve ethical responsibility and the attempt to prevent the control
over selfish passions which this involves from drifting into narcissism: justice must reorient our passions, not suppress them. It must
always unmask and transcend egocentrism, without submitting to
the seductive charm of that exercise, and thus falling into the wick-
edness of an absolute lust for self-satisfaction, power, and possession,
all of which are expressions of the imperialism of the *conatus essendi*.
The permanent danger menacing justice, making it a struggle "once
begun never done," is the pride rooted most deeply in private life, a
pride which does not look out for others and does not admit a need
to account for them. Even were our national, international, and world
society to return to the "one-for-the-Other," the "war of all against
all" would remain a permanent temptation. This makes it an urgent
part of the task of ethics to work within a just and peaceful society,
founded on responsibility and goodness, to anticipate and prevent
its fall back into the violent exercise of freedom (**AV** 217/184).

This means, above all, trying to limit and correct the evil which
can be founded by egocentric subjects (**ND** 59). Were it the case that
I stood eye-to-eye with only one Other, I would be defined strictly
and without qualification by his accusation, calling me to infinite
responsibility. I would be purely and simply for-him. And this would
hold even for the evil that he does to me: I am originally, or rather
"pre-originally" *not* his equal, wholly subject to him, responsible for
him all the way to standing in his place—"substituted" for him. My
resistance becomes justified only when the evil that is done to me

also strikes a third person, who is my neighbor. Out of duty to those third parties, both today and tomorrow, and out of duty to the categorical imperative promoting a just socio-political order—one which does as much justice as possible to all—one can not accept that a second person would suppress, neglect, exclude, or abuse a third person. When alterity takes the shape of an enemy and aggressor, the principle of respect for the otherness of the Other is no longer in effect. Instead, one must seek to know who is right and who is wrong, or who has acted justly and who not. For there are always people who act wrongly and unjustly toward others (**IEP** 5). This, of course, is the ultimate reason why sanctions against criminals—whether individuals, groups, or nations—are sometimes justified. It is the violence against third parties which justifies retribution, requiring us to call to account people or societies who act aggressively toward thirds (**DVI** 134/83-84). "Humility is undoubtedly the highest virtue—one must be like ground that is tread upon. But justice is necessary to protect the Others. One can not forgive violence in place of those who have undergone it and died by it. This brings us to the brink of substitution. To found peace in this world implies justice." (**ND** 59)

The Social Meaning of the "Jus Talionis"

It is against this background that Levinas gives a positive sense to the "jus talionis" of the Hebrew scriptures ("an eye for an eye, a tooth for a tooth"), but given such bad press since the rise of Christendom. First and foremost, it must be noted that this law does not promote personal revenge. In fact, revenge is something that the scriptures expressly forbid (*Lev* 19:18, *Gen* 4:15, *Deut* 32:35). "Tooth for tooth, eye for eye: this is not a way of indulging in the vengeance and cruelty which would somehow belong to human existence. This sort of inspiration is alien to the Jewish Bible. It comes from the pagans, from Macchiavelli and Nietzsche" (**DL** 195/146).

But if the law of compensation has nothing to do with revenge, then what is its proper meaning? Levinas points out that it is literally a *jus* talionis, in other words a rule which seeks *justice* via satisfaction. Someone who causes harm to another must give that other person satisfaction in a court of law, thus before a judge. In this respect, the law of compensation is plainly situated not at the interpersonal level of the face-to-face, but rather at the level of the third person, the social level. "The intention behind the apparent cruelty of the principle stated here by the Bible, is nothing other than justice. It makes up one part of a social order in which no sanction, however light it may be, falls outside legal judgment" (**DL** 195/146). The decision by and through the judge is more important than the noble outrage called forth by the crime. Where violence calls forth violence, there begins a chain reaction which it is the aim of justice to stop. Or better, this is the calling of justice, each time evil is committed. "Humanity is found in a person to the degree that he is able to call a deadly offence back to a quarrel taking place within the civil order, and to make punishment subordinate to making whatever reparations are possible, including the reform of the criminal" (**DL** 195/146).

Even a member of the SS has a face, which is also to say a right to justice, albeit a justice which will punish him and put an end to any further pursuit of his murderous plans (**MPR** 17-18). People like Klaus Barbie have a right to a judge and tribunal, even if their crimes are so terrible as to defy all humanity, far exceeding the possibility of a proportionate sanction. According to Levinas, it speaks honorably of the West that even in the face of such apocalyptic, incomparable cruelty it has managed to continue speaking about justice and judgment, which is to say the right to a defense and due process guaranteed in a climate of objectivity. Although there exists nothing in proportion to the outrages in recent memory, that very fact that justice can be discussed exposes their terrible inhumanity, so that one is no longer easily tempted by them—as are some in the younger generations which have not participated in them, but think they see some greatness, power, pride, and even humanity in it (**CI** 21).

With its command of punishment in proportion to the crime, the *jus talionis* serves above all to render insupportable all superficial thoughts about personal action (vigilanteeism, vendettas, revenge). Often, it is only "when we are paid in the same currency" and thus feel it in our own flesh that the true consequences of what we do to others finally dawns on us. In this sense, the *jus talionis* takes the evil between people most seriously. A human life is held to be unconditional; it is the most fundamental value. There is no possible substitution for it. "All eternity and all the money in the world can not heal the revilement done to a person. For this is a wound that bleeds forever, as if an equal suffering is necessary to stop up this eternal flow" (**DL** 196/147). In a society where only tenderness, love, and forgiveness would rule, the risk would be great of becoming to meek in the face of evil. Moreover, if one is too mild and too easy with remittance, one fails to take the crime and egocentric will to power which is its source seriously enough. If one pardons too quickly and too willingly, one denies both the responsibility belonging to each and all of us, and the fundamental evil of murder, with every form of denial of other people flowing from it.

LIMITS OF NON-RESISTANCE

In addition, Levinas points out how the total pacifism of a Jeremiah, who speaks of "turning the other cheek to him who has struck me, and bearing his insults" (*Lam* 3:30), or in the spirit of the gospel injunction to "offer no resistance... when someone strikes your right cheek, turn the other to him" (*Mt* 5:39; *Lk* 6:29), in fact can not be applied on the social level. So long as it is a mater of only one, unique Other, Levinas can accept this command to turn the other cheek. As "substitution," the one-for-the-other of responsibility also implies "expiation." I take the place of the Other, even if he irritates or persecutes me—but God save me from the obligation to make this the rule for everyday life! The question is only whether or how this can be realized in the sphere of socio-political justice. According to Levinas, the Scriptural principle of turning the other cheek to one's persecutor can not be generalized into tolerance of those who persecute not only me but also others, or third parties. For myself, I can indeed decide to forego an aggressive response to the aggression of my persecutor, and in this way put an end to the circuit of violence; but it is not possible for me to make this decision for or in place of others. I can not require others to turn the other cheek (**LAV** 118). Witnessing attacks or attempts to destroy a people, I can not leave those Others defenseless. They are Others who fall under my responsibility, even if they are my people and in that sense form an extension of myself. My own people and those who live beside me have no less right to justice and defense from persecution and violence as do those who are remote from me, and thus might more readily appear as homeless strangers. Levinas refers to this right to defense as an ethically necessary politics.

It is at this point that Levinas proposes his interpretation of Zionism and the state of Israel. He immediately rejects as false any messianic mysticism of the land which would give the Zionist state an ultimate and total meaning, as if the whole of messianism could be found there, and with that the whole Jewish problem resolved and the whole the calling of the Jewish people fulfilled. To refer to the Holocaust and say that God is with "us" in all circumstances, that is to say with the Jewish people, or with the Zionist state, is just as hateful and terrible as the *Gott mit uns* appearing on the hangman's noose. Such ideas lead one, both religiously and politically, into an ideology just as totalitarian as that of Hitler and his followers (**IEP** 3). For this reason, Levinas never admits a definitive or ultimate messianic significance for the Zionist state, though he also does not deny that there is a messianic dimension in it, as however is the case for any ethically founded and just socio-political order. Still, this political messianism can not be given the last word, but most be transcended by the messianism of the uniquely responsible ego. This implies that for Levinas, Zionism, apart from all ideological mystification, counts as a political idea with an ethical justification. Were Zionism solely my personal affair, were it only a matter of 'I-in-the-first-person' standing alone in the crowd, than I would certainly be free to renounce my right to self-defense. However, it is a matter here of more than 'my' affairs and 'my' right, but the affairs and the rights of an entire people. I have duties to my people, just as I stand accused before all Others. Consider the biblical account of Jacob, who with his two wives, Rachel and Lea, his children and slaves, and all his property, fled from his father-in-law Laban: when Laban caught up to him an asked for an explanation, Jacob said that he had to think of 'his entire household' (*Gen* 31). His 'household,' like that of anyone else, is the place where he can welcome his neighbors and offer hospitality (**LAV** 11). As a political idea, Zionism, the State of Israel, is legitimate to the degree that a political solution is necessary to bring an end to the arbitrariness threatening all Jews—that is to say, to protect against the danger of assimilation and thus disappearance of Judaism, including above all the bloodshed which for centuries has gone unpunished around the world. Hitler demonstrated once and for all that the Jewish people are exposed to a much greater danger than that of assimilation by or into a surrounding culture. It is for this reason that Judaism has need of a political identity and a state. And of course, this political solution is not possible *in abstracto*—as if indifferent to where or how it is accomplished—but requires a political unity with a Jewish majority and in a specific place. The fact that this has been situated in present-day Israel has everything to do with age-old memories which can not be separated from the place on earth to which they were first joined. The 'miracle of memory' must be brought together in the present moment with real things, or else risk being dissolved or evaporating in the contemporary world. Israel affirms its values in the places which have always been their cadre and milieu. Israel has already existed too long without the real Israel, even if the latter is far from comprising all of the intrinsic worth of Judaism (**MPR** 18).

Levinas thus offers an interpretation of Zionism according to which it is only political but at the same time very clearly so, displaying all the limits and restrictions belonging to any political state, as we will see. "For me, Zionism means a state in the full sense of the word, a state with a military and weapons, a military with powers of dissuasion and, if necessary, defense. Its necessity is ethical: this is indeed an old ethical idea, demanding precisely that we defend our neighbor. My neighbors and those who live alongside me are also my neighbors. One defends one's neighbor when one defends the Jewish people; and every Jew defends his neighbor all the more so when he defends the Jewish people" (**IEP** 4). Naturally, this does not mean that everything that the Zionist state does, even in the name of an ethically necessary politics of self-defense, is truly responsible—as became clear in, for instance, the massacres committed by the Israeli army in the Palestinian camps of Sabra and Shatilla, during September of 1982, from which Levinas distanced himself while at the same time upholding his overarching conception of political Zionism.

Let us now return from the particular to the general, or from concrete application to philosophical principle. According to Levinas, those of us who defend an Other with violent means must not fail to recognize that they have also attacked an Other, namely the violent aggressor. However, those who defend the Other against violent third parties do act justly. This implies, as surprising or even paradoxical as it may sound, that on the level of socio-political justice a certain degree of violence is sometimes *de facto* unavoidable and even—as final means—necessary. Note well: it is a matter here of defending an Other who is under attack, and not of defending myself (a situation addressed rather in the calls by Jeremiah and Jesus, to absolute love; WZE 151). To speak about justice is to introduce the idea of a struggle against evil. For Levinas, that struggle must include withholding from the idea of non-resistance to evil. While it is certainly questionable whether self-defense is always justified, it is also true that death comes in the person who threatens one's neighbor, and not always or only oneself: the person who menaces one's neighbor, rejecting or suppressing the neighbor's face, calls up violence just as surely as the one who menaces the one watching that terrible spectacle. Moreover, defense of one's neighbor against every sort of oppression is not only an individual task, but demands a structural, socio-political approach to the physical, psychical, economic, social, cultural, and political evil that people can do to one another. One is to avoid and overcome, or at least limit as much as possible 'violence against violence,' turning instead to negotiation, persuasion, and agreement. Still, one can not suppose *apriori* that there can never be a legitimate use of violence.

HUMANIZATION OF RETRIBUTION

However, this non-resistance to using the violence sometimes necessary to protect the third person from an aggressor is still not the last word in this matter. Nowhere does the dynamic principle of a self-overcoming, always improving justice hold more firmly than here, where it becomes necessary to employ violence against violence. We have already seen how penal law has the unmistakable social function of compensating and deterring. This compensation—or retribution, for in extreme cases it becomes violent—can not be an endpoint. In turn, society must seek a humane form of even this particular violence. The justice which protects the third person, when necessary with a weapon in hand, is also subject to correction. If not, sanction, violence, and war will provide themselves with a clear and peaceful conscience, erecting their own form of ethical legitimation or else appealing to historical necessity (**PP** 346/169). And they must not be permitted to settle into a definitive regime: their re-humanization is an ethical necessity. In this way, Levinas arrives at the conclusion that society itself, and not only individual conscience, must re-humanize the violence committed on the basis of its own assignment to justice for everyone, thus involving the protection of the weak—and without ever forgetting the injustices inflicted on third persons, or else become guilty of promoting a new, and perhaps even greater injustice. Through the fact that one must reckon with this face of this one person here and now, one also forgets the faces of the others. This can have serious consequences to be revoked or at least addressed thereafter. Striving for a humanization of the sometimes necessary compensation means standing up for "a truthful assessment of the somewhat complex system that this involves, and treating those who are judged by it with love" (**EFP** 97). Concretely, this might include abolishing the death penalty, as has occurred in a number of countries. Consequent with this vision of agreement between justice and love of neighbor, Levinas finds the abolishment of capital punishment essential and necessary (**PM** 175). This vision of an ethical duty to promote an 'improved justice' implies at the same time that the criminal is also a human being and also has rights: rights to humane treatment and living situation while in prison, including for instance a television in his cell. It is through this socially organized humanization that justice on the level of the third person becomes still more just (**EFP** 119).

Levinas also points out how the Jewish scriptures, even while articulating this law of retribution in the form of a *jus talionis* nonetheless call for its humanization. To begin with, the *jus talionis* in its strict sense ("an eye for an eye, a tooth for a tooth") is never formulated or applied as such in Jewish society. According to the Talmud (the Jewish interpretation and application of the Bible) punishment occurs as proportionate compensation, that is to say in money. We need not only a justice without passion, or one which is objective and neutral, but also one without an executioner. It is therefore necessary to be mild and humane when reckoning punishment for a crime. One can hardly take the life of a murderer on the pretense that the life he himself has taken is priceless! It is precisely because a society recognizes the irreparable seriousness of murder that it goes in search of repayment in the proper sense of the word. This is also true when one person puts out the eye of another, breaks her arm, or injures her body in any way: this must be repaid, and according to the essence of the *jus talionis*. What is extraordinary about this rule is to be found here, where one person is required to compensate for the lost economic worth of the injured body part, represented therefore as force, or power. Someone who has lost an eye is likely to have decreased income: in such a case, the offender must pay her social security, including the cost of the doctor and treatment until recovery; the offender must also pay for her loss of income, whether through loss of work or decreased productivity; and finally, according to the Talmud, the offender must also pay for the fact that she is less attractive, or that her dignity is tarnished. As Levinas admits, one can certainly be astonished at the idea of payment for this last category, but this can not change the fact that it is necessary to take some account of the (economic) damage done to another human being. Marx already referred to this sort of idea as "scandalous," and yet this economic calculus can support the real possibility of humanizing the inexorable hardness of a law enforcing retribution. It is an exceptionally important form of social humanization, and thus of a better justice in turn striving for an always better justice.

Nevertheless, it is important to avoid misunderstanding on this point. The Talmud leaves no doubt that murder is an remains an extremely serious and irreparable offense. This is clear in the formulation in which the Jewish tradition has always preserved the *jus talionis*. Levinas brings this out in connection with the subtle question posed by Chouchani, his master in reading the Talmud: why have we retained this formulation, rather going directly into talk of financial compensation? why, if compensation refers to money, does one say 'an eye for an eye?' rather than 'money for that eye'? His answer is that even if an offense has been 'made good' financially, nothing has in fact been exchanged. Otherwise, someone with enough wealth could rightly put out the eyes of many and then repay everyone for their losses. The king of Israel could have done this to all of his subjects; the Rothschilds could have done so to their workers, or perhaps to the entire world. In other words, to tamper with the strict formulation of the *jus talionis* would be to introduce a justice stratified by classes, so that not only would right and wrong have different content for those of different wealth, but also those with greater wealth could inflict suffering on those with less, and without a guilty conscience. For the strong, the world would remain a comfortable place, so long as they have sufficient nerve (**DL** 196/147). According to Levinas, the strict formulation of the *jus talionis* has been maintained in the Jewish tradition precisely in order to prevent the gentler or more humane side of justice from growing into a 'wide and easy avenue for the rich.' Still, this does not take away from the fact that money can and must play an important role in compensation. Such a humanization of justice is in fact one of the primordial functions of money, though of course this can be said only without forgetting the necessary restrictions and with an eye on the principle of reciprocal and proportionate compensation. In any case, there can be no economic quantity or financial value set on human life.

It is clear that this and every struggle for a better justice is possible only through inspiration and animation by the responsibility of the one-for-the-Other. It is through this fundamental goodness and mercy that justice for the third person becomes even more just, or better: that there takes hold a creative, courageous, and resolute drive for an ever improving justice. Mercy demands a politics of justice, which in turn demands mercy—a mercy which in fact must not be separated from this justice (**AS** 62). So long as love of neighbor is part of justice, there will always be an expectation and a demand for better justice. Since the goodness of the one-for-the-Other is the heart of justice, it cares for and seeks an "infinition" of justice, which perhaps gives prophetic witness to the Glory of the Infinite.

The "Small Goodness" Has the Last Word

The responsibility of one-for-the-Other also functions in another manner: as critical corrective of socio-political justice in the grace of small mercies, or small goodness (*la petite bonté*). In order to clarify this, Levinas begins from an analysis of the structural violence inherent to every socio-political order.

The Structural Violence of
Every Socio-Political Order

However necessary the socio-economic and political order may be for the third person, it also immediately introduces into love of neighbor a first violence which, properly speaking, does not come from the third person but rather the structure of society itself (**EFP** 97). It belongs to the intrinsic nature of even the most ethically inspired, just state or socio-political form of society that it runs a constant risk of submitting to this aspect. Wherever it takes shape in laws, establishments, and structures, it also displays an anonymous, objective, and alienating character. Levinas also refers to this as the "determinism proper to" every political structure (**LAV** 117). While it does have its origin in the ethically inspired free will, it also returns upon that will with a certain alienation. Its nameless and impersonal objectivity becomes the cause of the free subject's eventual inability to locate its original intentions there. Ethical intentions flow into it but are then closed off. Institutions obey a rational order in which the freedom established in responsibility no longer sees itself. The original will to justice no longer recognizes itself in the values it has taken up in order to resist its own decline (**LC** 266/17). This is certainly the case for those of us who have not participated in the work of bringing the prevailing socio-political structures and laws into being. It is these people who experience the distinction between ethics and politics most clearly. "The moral work of politics distinguishes itself from morality in the sense that comes first 'from outside' where it is added on to the moral intention and freedom of the individual, thus bringing about a liberation in which the individual might well recognize himself but of which he is not the true agent, a liberation in spite of himself" (**TMI** 269).

This 'heteronomy of the political' misforms and alienates the responsibility and justice which, however, lie at its root: "notwithstanding the rationality which the state and politics realize, we announce an oppression" (**TMD** 288). Left to itself, politics becomes a new tyranny. On the basis of its anonymous and objective power structure, the socio-political order exhibits a constant tendency toward "structural violence" (**TI** 230/252, 276/299-300). Here we come upon the paradoxical, or better, ambivalent and alienating nature of every socio-political structure (**LAV** 121): it is on one hand absolutely necessary if we are to also reach third persons with our peace-loving responsibility and goodness, while on the other hand, as order, institution, and structure, it also always implies "structural violence—a violence which comes from the structure as such. To be sure, one must always share and apportion, and one must know what A does to B and B to A. The ego, too, is caught up in this circle. The direct ego-Other relation is an asymmetrical relation, because I am responsible to the Other *without expectation of reciprocity*. However, this famous thesis in fact disappears behind the circuit of communal life. Here, equality and symmetry form a second moment tending to mask the first. This symmetry is a first violence from which flows all the other violence of politics. But as "rationality" or "wisdom of love," as ethical transcendence of the egocentric arbitrariness of the free subject, a transcendence rooted in the fundamental proximity animating all justice, the socio-political order must be described as "nonviolent," or rather as "peaceful"; it is not in a condition to "arm itself against the violence from which this non-violence lives" (**TI** 16/46).

In this sense, politics would seem to be bent by an internal contradiction. Through the structures it creates, politics subordinates people to other people, precisely in order to liberate them—which are also the principles and basic relations defended and incarnated by those in power. Anyone who abstains from cooperating with the state thus makes himself the accomplice of those dark and enslaving forces which the state exists to resist. Now, in the service of the state, one contributes to structural oppression, but when one turns against the state one serves the subterranean power flowing from egocentrism. This is the drama of all politics. The same socially and politically organized justice originating from the ethical appeal of the face eventually turns back against the face (**LAV** 120-121).

"Universal Reason" as Source of Structural Violence

What is the source of this tyranny by the socio-political order? According to Levinas, it is the universality of a "generalized Reason" (Hegel) of the state of socio-political order of society itself. However rational the political order may appear, individuals will eventually encounter violence in its objective universality, through which political institutions and laws try to define and determine them as precisely as possible.

Levinas finds a concrete illustration of this "oppressive" universality in "administration," or the socio-political "apparatus." "One can speak of oppression even in a completely just state, precisely because the subject's relation to universality, through which the subject is indeed (as subject) recognized but also "defined,' passes inevitably into administration" (**MBJC** 54). Administration, and the bureaucracy which belongs to it—even if they are of revolutionary and ethical origin—are by nature incapable of taking proper account of the truly unique, since they manage regulations, enforce laws, and found institutions which must consider all individuals equal and treat all individuals impartially. In the state, genre and sort return as regulative and operational categories. Everyone is considered and addressed by the same denominators, such as employer, employee, taxpayer, road user, student, and teacher, or more generally as citizen, all of which render people more or less similar instances of a same type or types, with the result that they can be compared and even exchanged. "Administration, that is to say the hierarchy by which the state exists and continues to exist, alienates the very subject who it is to preserve in his purity. In order to repel violence, one must appeal to violence. The subject no longer recognizes his own (ethical) will in the consequences of the 'vote' which brought them about" (**TH** 94/15). The administrative means by which the triumph of the responsible and just subject was to have been assured becoming the source of a new way to alienate that subject. Magistrates, as magistrates, place their "decisions" under the sign of universality, and as such can have no eye for the concrete Other in her unicity. This means that even the most well-intentioned and humane administration obscures the irreducible and transcendental human dignity of the unique Other, thus in fact degrading it (I 131/243).

Subjects function as elements of the globalizing calculations of the apparatus, through which it becomes possible the insert the rational order necessary for justice into the state. This is the price which individual subjects must pay. It is from this functionalizing order that they receive their "social being" and can occupy their place in the social "system." They therefore also conceive of one another through the concept of ideal necessities confronting and commanding them from all sides on the cultural, economic, social, and political level. On the socio-political level they are not what they truly are (according to their irreducible unicity or alterity), but instead play a role in a drama of which they themselves are no longer the authors. They are promoted, or better, degraded to forms or instruments of a homogeneous and rational social order which directs and fulfills itself from beyond their direct initiative. No one can truly find in his or her deepest heart the socio-political structures and laws that guide our behavior. In the epoch of common life, of impersonal universal reason, human beings are rather more "actors" than the "director." One plays a scripted role under the invisible direction of the anonymous determinism of the state. In this sense, social and political order is the work of finite subjects who betray their ethical projects in order to achieve them, which is to say that they do not actually command their own work. For such people, "fate"—to be taken literally as a far-off destination—consists in playing, at the right moment, a role in the growth of his culture and society, and not in embracing that entire process. Today one plays only the role of a "relative moment" in a system, and not the role of its "origin" (**DL** 125/93-94).

According to Levinas, we find an eminent and consequent incarnation of this political truth that fulfills itself in the anonymous and generalized order of the state, in the soviet communism of the Stalinist variety. This is not to say that he denies that the original inspiration of Marxist socialism derives from a recognition of our duties to and from the Other, though of course Marxism developed into quite another position than his own. Marxism asserts that we can save the Other if the Other demands what is rightfully his. Marxism invites the Other to make that demand for what I am duty-bound to give him. Still, even if this does differ from Levinas' conception of radical asymmetry between me and the Other, it does not necessarily incur condemnation. Before Marxism grew into a power-hungry struggle for revolution, it served the ethical intention of taking the plight of the "proletarian" Other as seriously as possible. Furthermore, it emphasizes the importance of the economic dimension of solidarity and responsibility from the very beginning. What is truly positive about socialism is that it opposes a responsibility expressed only in 'good words' rather than tangible deeds of economic assistance or the necessary socio-economic reforms. Nonetheless, it is impossible to overlook the "Stalinist disillusion" which, along with the discovery of the third-world, has scarred our post-war experience. Everyone is by now familiar with how the original generosity of Marxism was, under a Stalinist impulse, gradually perverted into an administrative and bureaucratic system with inward pretensions toward totalization and outward tendency toward usurpation. We have already seen how Levinas criticizes Stalinism as the definitive system. Here it is more a matter of how he brings out the continuity between Stalinism and every system as such. To be sure, we can rightly point to considerable and no doubt important differences between our own political system and Stalinism, freeing us from the great perversity of the latter. Still, we must not be too quick to rejoice in our good fortune, or to deny all complicity in the violence and oppression exercised by those in power and the ones who serve them. Without denying all of this— for history reminds us of it repeatedly—Levinas directs his attention mainly to the Stalinist-inspired soviet communism, as the consequent and extreme culmination of the socio-political system as such. In reality, Stalinist socialism, which promotes a democracy without parties via the disappearance of class-distinctions, represents nothing other than the political ideal of the whole of western philosophy, especially Hegel's rational idealism, with the single difference being that the conclusions derive from premises "to which our syllogisms hold fast 'without' conclusions" (**DL** [1963] 221). The implicit or explicit metaphysics to which, according to Levinas, western thinking always ultimately appeals, is nothing other than the ideal of Reason or of the universal rational order by which homogeneous development and progress are possible. "Western thinking, already long before Hegel, is accustomed to considering the State as the incarnation of Spirit. A state without contradictions is the realization of the humanity of man. It is Reason realized, and is Reason even in its becoming, which reveals itself progressively. The individual finds his highest fulfillment in the State" (**DL** [1963] 222). According to a political system that considers itself all-encompassing and "completely true," the individual with its anxieties and unrest belongs to the domain of illusion and ideology. The needs of subjective conscience count as symptoms of hysteria. The strictly personal and the intimate have no importance. When liberty, equality, and fraternity are considered at the level of heart or feeling, they are written off as expressions of an abstract, civil morality! For this thinking according to the universal Reason and Order of the State, there exists only an "objective" freedom that applies itself by and to the principles and norms of political rationality. For Stalinist communism, "soviet citizens, who have stupefied the world with their labor, can not be slaves. They are free according to an objective freedom to which Reason has introduced them— indeed, in spite of themselves (but what does that matter?)" (**DL** [1963] 222). For Levinas, most serious of all is the fact that we Westerners go along with this vision without even realizing it: one heeds this ideal of universality oneself, and as it is incarnated in the socio-political system (**DL** [1963] 223). Beginning from the western conviction that real freedom requires the "de-individualization of the individual," that is to say the agreement of the will with universal Reason, "the greatest spiritualists of our time take the view that the economic transformations of our world and the construction of an international industrial society will join humanity with universality in a single stroke" (**DL** [1963] 222). It is finally in this sense that Levinas claims that every socio-political form of society contains the seed of totalitarianism.

The Human Being Disappears in Its Own Works

As a second illustration of the structural oppression and violence of universality, Levinas points to the (economic) "work" (*l'oeuvre*). The condition for the possibility of reducing the unique subject to universal Reason, he contends, the economic product, or work. In the work one produces, one also exposes oneself. The worker expresses himself, but at the same time withdraws from the expression. Or better, according to Levinas' paradoxical formulation: "To approach someone from works is to enter into his interiority as though by burglary; the other is surprised in his intimacy, where, like the personages of history, he is, to be sure, exposed, but does not express himself" (**TI** 38/66-67). In a work, the maker is present in and through his default. This confers on him the "ontological status of the ego as third person" (**MT** 364); and "works signify their author, but indirectly, in the third person" (**TI** 38/67). The powers of the subjective will no longer coincide with one's own élan, or thrust, and thus no longer accompany his work to the very end. There is always a distinction between the producer and the product. At a certain moment, the producer no longer accompanies the product but remains behind. The self-transcendence and externalization occurring in the work remain only half accomplished. The will escapes the will. The independent subject does not completely comprise his own essence. A work is always in a certain sense a failed act. In it, I am not entirely what I want to be (**TI** 203-204/227-229).

Levinas designates this the "phenomenal" character of the work: "The *who* involved in activity is not *expressed* in the activity, is not *present*, does not attend his own manifestation, but is simply signified in it by a sign in a system of signs, that is, as a being who is manifested precisely as absent from his manifestation: a manifestation in the absence of being—a phenomenon." (**TI** 152-153/178). When one grasps someone by his works, that someone is surprised (*surpris*) rather than comprehended (*compris*). His labor masks him. "The phenomenon is the being that appears, but remains absent. It is not an appearance but a reality that lacks reality, still infinitely removed from its being. In the work, someone's intention has been divined, but he has been judged in absentia.... He has been understood like a prehistoric man who has left hatchets and drawings but no words" (**TI** 156/181). In this sense, Levinas refers to the work as a "symbol" which in its disclosure of a "signifier" at the same time conceals it. "The Other signals himself but does not present himself.

The works symbolize him. The symbolism of life and labor symbolizes in that very specific sense that Freud discovered in all our unconscious manifestations and in our dreams, and which is the essence of every sign, its primordial definition: it reveals only in concealing" (TI 151/176).

As symbol, the economic work thus also requires "interpretation" (TI 153/178). This implies that the product, due to the absence of the producer, can be understood otherwise than as the producer intended. Others separate the work from its maker and situate it in a new context, but without necessarily reckoning with the context originally intended. It is therefore possible to actually turn a work against its author. Levinas calls this the "counter-sense" (*contre-sens*) of the work (MT 365). He also connects this to the concept of "destiny" (*destin*) or "fate" (*fatum*). "The idea of *fatum* accounted for the reversal suffered by every heroism in a role. The hero finds himself playing a role in drama exceeding his heroic intentions, which, by their very opposition to that drama, hasten the accomplishment of designs foreign to them. The absurdity of the *fatum* foils the sovereign will. In fact inscription in a foreign will is produced through the mediation of the work, which separates itself from its author, his intentions, and his possession, and which another will lays hold of" (TI 202/227). Through his works, one becomes the pawn of destiny, which overtakes him coming from others. The "counter-sense" which takes over what results from a will when that will withdraws from that result depends on the will of the "survivors." "Fate is the history of the historiographers, accounts of the survivors, who interpret, that is, utilize the works of the dead. The historical distance which makes this historiography, this violence, this subjection possible is proportionate to the time necessary for the will to lose its work completely. Historiography recounts the way the survivors appropriate the works of dead wills to themselves; it rests on the usurpation carried out by the conquerors, that is, by the survivors..." (TI 204/228).

Against this background, Levinas speaks of an "ontological alienation" and a "first injustice" that one undergoes in and through one's works. He refers to this alienation as specifically "ontological" because it is inherent to the work as such. The will does not have control over the full history of its own wishes because the work only points to its absence. He refers to this as an "injustice" because the original intention of the producer is not respected when others, that is to say, survivors give the work a meaning which is not only new but sometimes even contrary to that which the producer intended (**MT** 365).

This clearly illustrates how history can only be an economic history. The manner in which the will plays a role in history—a role that he or she may not wish—reveals the limits of subjectivity, and both in its interiority and its ethical unicity. The will is in the grip of events which will appear only to the historian. And it is precisely by means of works that historical events build ever greater connections. Without works, "wills" do not make history. History, the sole place in which the identity and ethical unicity of each subject is always plastic, always a mute product, can manifest itself, is necessarily material and not spiritual. The phenomenal, symbolic, and "non-expressive" character of the work is what comprises its value as commodity (**TI** 151/176). The fact that in the work the will escapes itself and no longer controls itself, implies that the others can master that work, acquiring it, buying and selling it, exchanging it or trading for it (**TI** 203-204/228). This returns us to the "inter-significance" or "exchange value" of money. In activity occurring with or through money, a work loses its "personal" significance, that is, its reference to the producer, in order to take on the "general" meaning of goods and commodity, which in turn permits it to be integrated into an individual's project of existing, whereby it receives a new specific meaning (**MT** 372).

This would seem to show that the socio-political order of human subjects can be achieved and maintained only through the economy of works. Neither the intimacy of interiority nor the selflessness of ethical unicity can escape it. The political system can take aim only at what people "do," thus at their works. It can apply itself to regulating relations between subjects only to the degree that these relations follow a tangible course of objective mediation by quantitative actions. The socio-political structure "realizes its through works" (**TI** 151/176). This "quantifying" approach to subjects through their works makes possible the rational universality of the State and of every socio-political form of society—both *intra*nationally and *in-*

*ter*nationally, since it is then unnecessary to take any account of the most subjective intentions of each unique individual. After all, these intentions are no longer directly present in the work. In this way, socio-political order promotes "a humanity of interchangeable people, of reciprocal relations" (**TI** 274/298). This is what makes possible the universal applicability of laws and regulations through which an equal justice for everyone can be achieved. But at the same time, this also involves a structural injustice committed against the human subject and her individual intentions.

The Abiding Necessity of "Small Goodnesses"

It is necessary not only to establish this fundamental ambiguity in every socio-political order—promoting justice, committing injustice—but also to consciously seek and preserve it from collapsing into totalization (**AS** 62). This means that one must always go beyond every new socio-political order with the ethical responsibility of each one ego for the separate and concrete Others. Inspired and impressed by Vassili Grossmann's *Vie et Destin*, Levinas calls this the need for "small goodnesses" between people. Grossmann's book describes the situation in Europe during the time of Hitler and Stalin, a time in which society became completely de-humanized and disintegrated through a terror of the camps under both Hitler and Stalin, a time ruled by a complete lack of respect for the human person. For eight hundred pages, the reader is confronted with absolute desolation and perversion. Grossmann no longer sees any horizon, any hope for the salvation of the human race. In particular, he describes the shock of Stalinism, which in fact emerged from a revolutionary struggle for human freedom. Stalinism testifies to the definitive end of a specific hope, namely the socialist hope to support and promote charity within an established regime. According to Grossmann, the slide of socialism into Stalinism represents the greatest spiritual crisis experienced by modern Europe. And what is especially tragic about this is the fact that Stalinism has its origins in the noble Marxist struggle for recognition of the Other, as we have already seen. In this respect, Stalinism differs fundamentally from Hitlerism, which came into existence out of the immorality of a racist lust for power and a merciless acceptance of the effort of being and the "Same" as the sole criterion for recognition of the other person, community, and society. As totalitarianism, Hitlerism and Stalinism are equally terrible, but whereas Hitlerism rests on a denial of ethics, Stalinism has roots through Marxism in a deep ethical ground and thus a hope for humanity. Convinced of the importance and need of the struggle for the proletariat, Marxism sought a regime without evil and in which to accomplish that goal. And the regime of charity became the terror of Stalinism.... Grossmann's book presents this Stalinist perversion as the greatest and indeed irreversible betrayal of humanity. Written by someone who had once shared an enthusiasm for what was lost there, the book is therefore marked by a deep despair and pessimism. Everything is lost. According to Grossmann, Stalinism demonstrates that every political organization has a fatal tendency to move toward de-humanization. And nothing can be done about it. The perversion of every political organization and state is inevitable. There is no change of regime which can truly put an end to this drama. The "system of salvation" is impossible (**RA** 15).

For Levinas, what is most remarkable in all of this is that there nonetheless remains something which the regime never extinguishes—the small goodness, the goodness without regime. Grossmann's book contains a long monologue by a certain Ikonnikov, who expresses the author's ideas. Ikonnikov places every rational organization, with its ideology and plans, mercilessly in doubt. For him, goodness as a regime, as an organized system and a social institution, is completely impossible. Every attempt to organize the human fails. Ikonnikov designates the only thing that remains the "small goodness," the goodness of everyday life and everyday people, and thus a goodness without witness, escaping every ideology. Ikonnikov also calls this a "goodness without thinking," since it falls outside of every system, religion, and social organization. It is completely gratuitous, mad, and therefore also eternal. It deserves special attention that this goodness is accomplished by those who we tend to call the weak or marginal. This is why it is so vulnerable to evil, which is much stronger. Small goodnesses are powerless and fragile, like the morning dew; as acts of events, they have all the appearance of trying to extinguish flames consuming the entire world with something as small and banal as a syringe... (**EPP** 125-126). Beyond all that it reports of the terrible violence in the camps, Grossmann's book is also strewn with small, isolated miracles of goodness taking place in the most inhuman of conditions. In the awful history of Europe's dissolution, the small goodness "without regime" have stood fast. Far from having been overrun, they survive as the only thing left. Hence does the book end with an account of the siege and defense of Stalingrad. The Germans had been beaten back. The Germans taken prisoner were required to empty the cellars beneath what had been Gestapo headquarters. This included removing the bodies of those whom the Gestapo had tortured and killed. A terrible scene ensued. A German officer, the most hated of the group of prisoners, was threatened by an unruly mob. The Russians screamed hateful things into his face. One woman was angrier than all the others. But then something completely unexpected happened. Precisely this same woman produced her last scrap of bread and gave it to that officer. This is a truly dramatic moment: this was the most unhappy, indeed furious person there. And yet, there still occurred the small goodness of person to person, a deed completely outside any system (**EFP** 133-135).

For Levinas, too, goodness is the greatest of miracles, and already long before his reading of Grossmann's book, as we find throughout his first master work, *Totalité et Infini* (**TI** 4/34, 76/103, 158/182-183, 225/247, etc.). This small goodness "above every system" can and does bring out the fact that unicity is grounded in election, in the shocking premise that I am I only through my election by the Other. Through my heteronomous responsibility, I am this one who must answer and who can not ask a second person to do so in my place. This election to a unique and irreplaceable role of responsibility is thus the true principle of individualization. This is the elected one's role, or rather her calling (**VA** 98). The ego established in and by responsibility must find what socio-political justice does not and can not find.

In a beautiful text, Levinas offers the following formulation of the necessity of small goodness which not only precedes the state but also comes after it (**EFP** 98): "There are, if you will, tears that a state functionary (or functionary of any other socio-political order) does not see, and can not see: the tears of the Other. In order for business

to function well and run smoothly, it is absolutely necessary to affirm the infinite responsibility of everyone, for everyone, and to everyone. In such a situation (of socio-political order), there is need of
individual consciences, for only they can see violence, the violence
flowing from the effective functioning of Reason itself. We must defend subjectivity against a certain disorder flowing from the Order of
that universal Reason. In my view, the promotion and defense of
subjectivity rests not on the fact that its egoism would be holy, but
on the fact that only the ego can see the "secret tears" of the Other,
tears brought about by the efficient function of the socio-political
hierarchy. Consequently, subjectivity (of the responsibly established
ego) is indispensible for the achievement of this non-violence which
the state (and every socio-political order) seeks, but while also passing by the particularity of the ego and the Other" (**TH** 102-103/16-
17).

In other words, no socio-political order can have the last word,
even if it does remain ethically necessary for the realization—here
and there, today and tomorrow—of responsibility for everyone. This
distinguishes Levinas from Grossmann, who does not believe in the
state or in politics. While goodness is exceptionally important and
forms the basis for everything else, it still must become justice in and
through a socio-political order. Levinas is not a pessimist, like
Grossmann. He continues to believe in the ethical necessity and positive meaning of socio-political justice, on the condition, however,
that it not become the alpha and omega of everything else. In this
sense, Levinas can be said to defend an "ethics without an ethical
system" (**EFP** 135). The individual ethical responsibility of the one-
for-the-Other is wholly irreplaceable, and not only as origin but also
as overcoming and fulfillment of socio-political justice and peace.
Due to the inevitable inattentiveness of the socio-political order to
supremely individual need of the unique Other, goodness must not
only guide politics toward an ever better justice, but where necessary
it must supplement or replace it. Whereas Hobbes had said that the
state is built on a delimitation of violence rather than of love of neighbor, Levinas develops out individual ethical responsibility limits for
that state and politics (**EI** 85-86/89-90). And whereas, for his part,
Levinas does recognize the legitimacy, or perhaps better, the inevita-

bility of a certain objective and structural violence—a violence without which justice for everyone would be impossible—he nonetheless argues with equal force that this necessary violence must not only be limited as much as possible, but also exceeded by the unique responsibility of the ego which comes to each of us "separately" and in the name of the unique Other. Justice can not be detached from love of neighbor. Levinas is thus opposed to both an abstract justice and an objectivistic or "pure" politics (**LAV** 120), which are ruled by the thought that a good general principle is can be applied everywhere.

The responsibility of the one-for-the-Other strives to do justice to each separate case. This brings Levinas to plead for a "noble casuistry" (**LAV** 121). As he sees it, the value of casuistry consists in the way it takes constant account of this one, concrete case before it here and now. Or better, it considers people and situations not as particular applications of a general principle, but in their irreducible and unrepeatable unicity. Of course, Levinas does not deny that casuistry has had (or still has) a pejorative reputation, and mostly through its own fault. Some have appealed to it hypocritically, or even abused it in order to, as it turned out, either defend themselves or pass judgment on others. It will always be possible to represent a concrete situation with specific attention only to certain details (and lack of attention to others) in a manner lending itself to ideological justification of a biased judgment. Nevertheless, casuistry is an affair of very great importance, for it is essentially a search for an adequate basis to render judgment, understood to remain within the limits of the relation and actions of a unique situation. It is above all a recognition of the fact that the being I find before me is completely now, or *hapax*: someone who is there but once, here and now. In this respect, ethical casuistry is an eminent precaution against every form of ideology and reduction which claims to deduce each concrete event from a more general principle—in other words, bad casuistry (**LAV** 122). However necessary it may be, the general scope of laws, submitting each of us to a bureaucratic standpoint, fall fearfully short here. This is why judgment must not be rendered by an objective and purely institutional regulating mechanism, but judges—by concrete, individual people. Between the law and those to whom it is applied, a judge is an absolute necessity—a thinking and deliberating ego, someone who can enter into a unique relation with the Other. And this in turn is precisely why we need individual consciences who in their corporeal affectivity are sensitive and vulnerable to the suffering of the separate and unique Other, and so compensate for the objective and inevitable lack in socio-political provisions (**WZE** 150-151).

THE SIGNIFICANCE OF HUMAN RIGHTS IN AN OPEN HISTORY

For a complete account of Levinas' analyses of an ever improving justice and the small goodness, it remains only to connect them to his philosophy of history and the place occupied there by human rights.

Let us begin with his vision of history. Now, the simple fact that Levinas defends the ethical necessity of an ever improving justice as transcendence of the existing justice certainly does not guarantee that this actually occurs, or that justice and goodness will triumph in the end. Levinas himself knows evil all too well to suppose so. His entire philosophy is marked by, or better a reflective expression of the trauma of the absolute Evil of antisemitism and Auschwitz caused by Hitler and his followers (**DL** 285/221). Anyone who lives in this world with his or eyes truly open knows perfectly well that honor and charity are constantly threatened and often even annihilated by the inhuman necessity of "be-ing" which drives us all, as well as economy, social reality and politics as a whole, including the ideologies that grew out of noble inspiration but whose corruption marks the great tragedy of the twentieth century (**RA** 15). There is no biological or psychical need in us to act justly or serve the good. There is, in contrast, only an ethical command which, by uprooting us, can leave us tumbling in the wind. Even if there is an "ethical impulse" virtually requiring us to recognize the Other as our neighbor, each of us nonetheless possesses an equal capacity to refuse or deny the absolute responsibility which that recognition implies. Or better: in order to be realized, the good must overcome the iron laws of being and the resilience of the individual effort to be. And this is certainly not self-evident. The fact that the "for-the-Other" is, as Levinas contends, a divine trace is not enough to insure good fulfillment of this divine call. We must harbor no illusions: the law of being, of the strongest, often takes precedent over goodness. And even when it does not, it can reclaim it at any moment. In this respect, Levinas' philosophy of history is plainly without an optimistic vision of its end. It is just as likely or possible that it will end badly as that it will end well. Our own spirited wish for such a good end is far from guaranteeing that this will indeed suffice to bring about the triumph of goodness and justice. Prior to the twentieth century, most major religions clung to the promise of a happy end, including not only Christianity, but also Judaism, with its vision of a history of salvation fulfilled in messianic eschatology. But God remained silent during the Shoah, a fact which deprives us of the right and the means, since then, to assume that everything will come out well. According to Levinas, this is an experience as important as what happened on Mt. Sinai, where God did speak. Since Auschwitz, the promise that it is the good which will triumph is no longer credible (**MPR** 14).

This forces us to ask whether the evil witnessed in the Shoah does not require us to abandon the good in favor of Evil, and live henceforth like the Nazi's. After Auschwitz, what reason can there be for ethics? Should we not bow down before the overwhelming power of Evil, as the irresistible tide of history? Levinas is convinced that ethics retains its force and pertinence, even after the radical failure of ethics. This is, to begin with, our highest freedom, in which the real newness of humanity reveals itself and awakens to wonder. The great event of history and of salvation history is the breakthrough of the "otherwise then being" in the pure persistence of the being in its being. The truly human lies in the disruption of the *conatus essendi*, the struggle for life that sucks into the stream of evil and war. The real wonder of the Human lies in the placing in question of the "being for me," so that the call echos in a "being for the Other." In the possibility of "dis-interest," in this goodness, a human being becomes truly human. The animality of being that is considered as if rational is thus unmasked as irrational, so that the gratuity of goodness can appear as the new rationality, as rationality par excellence, in short, as peace: reason all the way to peace among (all) people. This goodness is also the only thing that is always possible, so that all despair and fatalism must be considered a priori to come from evil. This still does not imply naive optimism about the success of justice. It is precisely our human assignment, our task as creatures, to learn to live in this uncertainty, and not to allow our ethical commitments depend on the prospects of satisfying them. Auschwitz invites us to think of an ethics independent of a happy end. After Auschwitz, ethics certainly remains possible, but we must accomplish it without promises.

In the domain of religion, this implies for Levinas a "piety without assurances," religion without consolation. Those who proclaim an eschatological assurance or reward from heaven introduce the dangerous idea of an ethics which is meaningful only if there is such an assurance or reward. According to Levinas, this means that we should refrain from "preaching." For the messianic future to have worth, we must accept that ethics is meaningful without the promise of a Messiah (**EI** 122/114). However, the fact that Auschwitz has deprived us of the right to appeal to the God of promises still does not mean that we should give up the God of Mt. Sinai. That God has already spoken as He who gave us the Decalogue. Henceforth, we must obey those commandments, but without assurances either that our ethical comportment will be repaid or that history will end in a triumph of the good. Again, from the fact that God did not speak at Auschwitz, and that we now know that we can not be certain of transcending evil, it does not follow that we should give up our attempt to bring ethics to fulfillment. The trauma of Auschwitz does not direct us to act against the injunctions of the Torah, becoming murderers, thieves, liars, racists, or misanthropes. Ethics retains its meaning, but without a salvation history. In this sense, the Torah, as the basic ethical law, more important than a well-defined, though imperfect idea of God (**MPR** 14).

Levinas does not fail to pose the question of whether we can "preach" this ethics without covenant to other people. "It is easier to tell myself that I must believe without assurances than to ask this of another. This is the idea of asymmetry. I can demand of myself what I can not ask of the other" (**PM** 176). Can one truly promulgate the idea of a "piety without assurances" and an "ethics without a future" without offering any comfort or security whatsoever? It is clear that Levinas has a great aversion to all preaching—"I am neither a preacher nor the son of a preacher," he notes (I 137/247), with or without promises. One thing remains paramount: history must be borne by the saintly and the just who, without assurances—and if only for a moment—break with the relentless flow of the history of being, and found the Human in unconditional goodness. Realists might call this an "illness" (*maladie*), but it is certainly no evil (*mal*).

Even if one understands this ethical saintliness as "the folly of the cross," which in a certain sense it is, this does not take away from the fact that it has the first and last word in all things—and not as word, philosophy, poetry, or proclamation, but as simple deed of goodness, such as we saw embodied in Mother Teresa, for whom Levinas had a great admiration. Mother Teresa took the simplest and most direct path to other people. She concerned herself with the all the misery of the flesh, without deference to personal identity, religion, or social status. Yet, however beautiful such behavior is, it can not be displayed or disseminated, for then it becomes both suspicious and irritating. Real exercise of goodness stands in complete disproportion to all possible words and preaching about self-denial. It is a scandal to confuse love of neighbor with the poetry that sometimes celebrates it. Or to remain silent about all the crime committed allegedly in the name of that love. It is a terrible betrayal to make acts of charity into an argument (**LAV** 112-115).

It is through this idea of goodness as transcendence and fulfillment of justice that Levinas explicates his own contribution to human rights and community. We have already seen how the core of human rights is to be found in recognition of the rights of the Other. In this respect, they are therefore a particular and proper expression of goodness. And as such, they are not only the basis, but also the correction and completion of a just society. Human rights do not merely begin from just society, but also transcend it. Those of us who think and act according to our call to promote human rights, thus for example standing up for the rights of the marginal and alienated, in fact do more for humanity than could any socio-political structure in itself, since such structures are by definition immune to a sense of the unique identity of each Other. In our increasingly international and structurally organized society, those who live from a sense of human rights make it possible for all responsible people to orient themselves to the necessary surplus of goodness for every Other.

But there is still more. Such people, precisely by exceeding and thus critiquing the existing state of affairs, also fulfill a particular function *within* the system of justice which is already socially and politically organized. Or better, they do so simply by acting from consciousness of the fact that justice is never just enough (**EFP** 98). And from this position, one demands that basic rights not yet actually stipulated or realized are now recognized and translated into the socio-political order. These rights and this way of defending them belong essentially to the "liberal" social order itself, insofar as it is an order where politics is not definitive or total. Even if human rights do not coincide with the presence of a government and are thus without any direct political or statistical function, they are nonetheless recognized within the (liberal) political structure as an indispensible establishment parallel to the written law. It is precisely this recognition within the structure that makes a state "liberal." To provide a specific institutional place for human rights is to accept the fact that it is not the socio-political order itself that proclaims the first and last word, but simply love of neighbor. A politics that accepts human rights also submits to critique by or in light of these rights, so that justice can always be improved. From the perspective of human rights, which do not coincide with the regime itself, it is always possible to put one's finger on the wound of injustices. By speaking up against failure to respect human rights, one places the existing political system radically in question, or breaks it open to still greater justice. This commitment is thus an expression of how love transcends justice, at least when justice is identified with a system of procedures and judgments. The call to respect human rights reminds us that we do not yet have a socio-political system which is perfectly just (**EFP** 119).

Human rights therefore have a critical and prophetic character. They strike against all self-complacency or secure conservatism, literally calling—provoking—us forward to strive after complete justice, and without falling into totalizing systems. In this way, they hold open the future of an ideal society. We might call this utopism, insofar as it aims at what can not be fully realized. But at the same time, it is an effective utopism, since it directs all of our ethical comportment toward justice and goodness. And while this utopia is indeed unreachable, that fact does not stand in the way of critically judging existing situations and structures, or of keeping an eye on the relative progress which can be made. This utopian thinking does not condemn all other thinking, but instead catalyzes it, so that we are always dynamically open, or re-opened to the future. Without the utopia of human rights and goodness, the ethical life is impossible (**PM** 178).

Finally, Levinas indicates that not even human rights as instance for transcending the state from within the state can have the final word on the surplus of goodness. While they are indeed constantly refined and re-worked, they nevertheless remain within the order of general solutions and abstract formulas. This of course means that as such they can never do what is accomplished by goodness itself, in its care for the unique Other through the concrete deeds which he calls small goodnesses. The small goodness is, in other words, irreplaceable. It alone is disposed *hic et nunc* to respond the unique face of the Other with concrete deeds as a unique and adequate answer (**EFP** 98). It is also through this real, small goodness that there is still trust in the future—a trust without guarantees, to be sure—for even absolute Evil is powerless against it. Were everything else to collapse so that it would appear impossible for any socio-political system to conquer Evil, there would still remain small goodnesses (**RA** 15-16). This, then is the last word—and literally so, including within the philosophy of Levinas, with its discussion of justice, peace, and human rights. The saintliness of goodness, the priority of the Other over myself, is the only thing which can never be put in question (**AS** 72). Even if this "extravagant saintliness" (**PP** 346/169) is no doubt also a difficult saintliness, one which can not be proven by the statistics which only measure self-interest and its results (**AEG** 30), still it is the unshakable foundation of the humane as a real possibility, notwithstanding the betrayal that can always beset it once again (**RA** 16).

Conclusion
Jerusalem and Athens:
The Wisdom of Love Needs
the Love of Wisdom

Levinas' philosophy of responsibility, peace, justice, and human rights is far from simplistic or easy. It is a thinking which tries to both disclose foundations and, on that basis, do justice to interpersonal and social reality. Above all, his views on the relationship between love of neighbor and justice for human rights offers interesting potential for new and paradoxical ways of thinking about political peace and human rights. While the law and justice are born out of love of neighbor, they nonetheless bear a kind of violence in them—a fact which Levinas designates with the paradoxical remark that love of neighbor gives birth to violence. It is precisely for this reason that love of neighbor must always return to transcend justice. This also goes for our relation with the Other, which is born in and as love of neighbor (**DAH** 60). That relation becomes economic and socio-political peace only through the appearance of the third person. But this is a peace which is never without violence. This why it too, in its turn, must be transcended by the "small peace" of goodness. This same dialectic goes for human rights, as well. According to Levinas, human rights are born out of responsibility-to-and-for-the-Other, which emerges precisely in the rights belonging to the weak and vulnerable Other. When they are defined primarily by a right to freedom and then bound to the self-interested effort to be, or as Levinas puts it, the "Same," then they become sources of violence. But when they are centered on the Stranger who is a unique Other, they become the source of peace, proximity, and fraternity. With the arrival of a third person, however, these human rights must be translated into social, economic, juridical, and political structures, laws, and institutions. As such, they become once again the source of violence, conflict, and new injustices. Therefore, in their purely non-political formulation, they must transcend the social, economic, juridical, and political forms which they receive, and even place them in question, so that the rights of the Other person can be taken to heart anew. This is the ultimate, prophetic significance of human rights, as the foundation of peace and justice. For their realization, we do not need propaganda or preaching, but just and holy people, people who are, in the literal sense of the word, "extra-ordinary." They and they alone support the world, though of course their remarkable deeds do not possess any magical power to change the entire world and its history, carrying it to a happy end (**LAV** 116-117). Such are the madmen and naive souls courageous enough to lay down their birthright in service of the Other (**VA** 102). And even if they are not assured of having the last word in this history of ours, this does nothing to change the fact that they are "the light of our world."

THE BIBLE AND GREECE

This wisdom of love, still in need of the Greek love of wisdom in order to realize itself at the socio-political level, is the wisdom of the Jewish Bible. In Levinas' perspective, the wisdom of love is prior to the love of wisdom of love, but the two must come together Europe is Jerusalem and Athens, the Bible and Greece. Yet these two sources do not converge; the one is prior to the other (**EFP** 114). This order is not to be understood purely formally, as a simple matter of (temporal) succession. The two sources are bound together by an inner "intrigue" according to which the Greek love of wisdom receives new meaning and an ethical foundation from the biblical wisdom of love not found as such in Greek thought.

According to Levinas, left to itself, Greek thinking begins from the question of how to overcome the conflictual plurality and irrationality of "Opinion," or *doxa*, and passion. That is, it is animated by a desire for unity and autonomy. Furthermore, Greek thought has always held that the only way to achieve these things was obedience to Reason, which is general and all-encompassing. This vision of Reason can be found throughout western thinking, including that of Kant, where he defends the priority of practical reason (**DAH** 44). This obedience of the will to Reason is also to resolve all violence, both subjective and interpersonal. After all, this obedience is based on the insight and evidence that it holds not only for me, but everyone and equally. Hence does the subject agree, submitting itself to the law of Reason, making it its own inner law (thus also defining humanity by the power of understanding). Hence, too, can many people, with their very plurality threatening to being conflict, enter into mutual agreement but without compelling one another: all are subject—or, proceeding by insight and argumentation, *subject themselves*—to the one, universal Truth. This general rationality is also the foundation for politics, as we have already seen. Fundamentally, the basis for this love of universal wisdom, including the general laws and structures of the "polis," is and remains (a self-interested desire for) autonomy.

When Levinas gives priority not to autonomy or the unity of the "Same," both of which are defined by obedience to Reason, but instead to the face and command which go out from the radical otherness of the Other, then everything which follows must receive a new meaning. When it is a matter of the wisdom of love, as command, needing the love of wisdom as universal truth of the polis in order to reach not only the second person, the Other, but also the third person, near and far, present and future, then the foundation of Greek wisdom is no longer the autonomy of the Same—no longer the relation between the ego and Reason—but the heteronomy of a responsibility conferred on me by the face of the Other. The entire range of what we have called noetic and practical totalization is, upon the arrival of the third person, taken up anew, but revalorized, though without a complete re-orientation and purification (thus requiring constant vigilance and the movement of transcendence). However, they are no longer grounded in the axiology of self-interest, but rather that of holiness (**AS** 60). Here, then, is the site of Levinas' ethical enrichment of Greek wisdom.

A STRICTLY PHILOSOPHICAL POSITION

When he says that this enrichment privileges Jerusalem over Athens, Levinas does not mean that he merely leaves philosophy and takes up a Jewish theology rooted in the Bible, where a religious and ethical authority is revealed to us. The priority of the Other and of the wisdom of love is not an a priori for all thinking and simply extracted from the Bible, but an insight that announces itself in the name of experience and reflection, and that Levinas therefore refers directly to the test of phenomenology, which opposes any and all apriori criteria. He also states repeatedly that the priority of the ethical is asserted from a strictly philosophical position—as is, or was, the case with Kant before him. For while Kant did found the primacy of practical reason through a traditional analysis of reason—a founding that, in Levinas' work, goes beneath that reason—it remains the case that Kant did indeed place ethics first. With regard to the history of philosophy, it is this elevation of practical reason over theoretical reason that marks something really new in Kant. In this respect, Kant's work represents a challenge not only to change one's life but also to philosophize differently; what is revolutionary touches not only life itself, but the way we think about, especially where we try to relate theory and ethics.

It is clearly within this strictly philosophical line that Levinas situates himself, though of course his method is much closer to that of phenomenology than to Kantian transcendental philosophy. Note that his philosophical works never refer to biblical or Talmudic texts for "proof," but at most to illustrate an insight which is founded philosophically. A philosophical truth can never be based on the authority of a verse. The biblical verse "Thou shall not kill" is central in Levinas' philosophy and recurs frequently, but he tries to justify it on strictly phenomenological grounds (**AEG** 29). And in order to avoid causing any misunderstanding himself, he always distinguishes sharply between his philosophical texts and his so-called Jewish writings, going so far as to publish them at different presses: one publishes only his Jewish, or confessional texts, while the other publishes the purely philosophical texts (**EFP** 111). He explicitly states that Levinas the philosophical author is not the Levinas who applies himself gladly to commentary and exegesis of Jewish texts (**AEG** 29).

The Universal Scope of the Command
"Thou Shall Not Kill"

This does not take away from the fact that he remains joined to what, following Alphonse De Waelhens, he calls "pre-philosophical," or "natural" experiences (**EI** 19/9). In this sense, he is far from either denying the biblical sources of his thinking, or concealing his reading of the Bible and his reliance on sacred Scripture and texts from the Jewish tradition (**AS** 73-74). Still, even when beginning from these texts, such as in his many stimulating Talmudic readings, he remains the philosopher he was first trained to be. After all, his philosophical formation had already been completed when, in 1946, he began intensive study of the Talmud, under his "extraordinary teacher," Chouchani. Accordingly, his relation to the Talmud was bound to, and did, remain both European and, indeed, philosophical. It was for this reason that he never wished to consider himself a true specialist in the Talmud, but instead a philosopher who happened to read it. With this attitude, he situated himself in the line of Talmudic thinking itself, with its methodical, peculiar, and sometimes even whimsical but nonetheless reflective wisdom aimed at bringing the confessional particularity of the Bible to bear on the universal task of "instructing" the spirit (**SaS** 7-9/91-92).

This explains why his relation to those texts is never devotional—as if they were religious metaphors within a symbolic-confessional universe—even if he does have all respect for those who do, as well as doing so himself, as a believing Jew, in his everyday life. In a Talmudic and philosophical spirit, he considers such texts as the sources of thinking or, more strongly, as their own form of thinking. In other words: what the text says is not true because it is in the Bible or Talmud, but it is in the Bible or Talmud because it is true. "When someone refers to me as a Jewish thinker, this is not something that shocks me in itself. I am Jewish and I occupy myself with specific Jewish texts, contacts, and traditions—this, I certainly do not deny. But I protest against the formula [Jewish thinker] when I am considered as someone who binds concepts, based on whichever tradition, to religious texts without taking the effort of submitting them to philosophical critique" (**EFP** 110). According to Levinas, it is necessary to distinguish two ways of reading a verse. The first of these consists in appealing to tradition and accepting its premises but without any afterthought or without rendering an account of the presuppositions on which that tradition depends. In such a case, one also makes no effort to make characteristic forms of expression and properties of language accessible to the uninformed reader or listener. A second way of reading consists in a strict reflective consideration which prefers not to immediately reject the text's suggestions, but accepts them from a philosophical standpoint and then pursues them, asking whether they can be justified by what they and their way of thinking present us with. Following this line, Levinas seeks a text's "objectively communicable intelligibility" (**EFP** 110). He is convinced that the verse, as an expression of a quite human and not exclusively religious culture, can possess a deep rationality or, again, is perhaps already thinking itself. For him, the Bible is the human fact of the human order, and consequently completely universal (**AEG** 177).

In our time, the text of Scripture is too quickly rejected on the ground that it lies within a specific confession. One shrugs it off without having yet listened to it, and certainly without having had the chance to hear in it the echo of a thinking at least as radical and "founding" as, for example, that of the fragments we possess of the pre-Socratics. There are situations in which a biblical verse, while restricted within philosophy to the role of illustration or suggestion, gives rise to an idea which immediately gathers sufficient power to guide even philosophical thinking—and not merely because it was found in the Bible, but due to the fact that it is exceptionally recognizable and thinkable (**EFP** 111). Levinas' primary example comes from the Decalogue: "Thou shall not kill." As he himself notes, the Bible and the Talmud frequently state that the ethical, the Torah as ethical command to love, justice, and freedom, represents "the ultimate intelligibility of the human and even of the cosmos" (**SaS** 10/93). But this converges perfectly with his own strictly philosophical thinking, which is easy to understand recalling that his thinking is determined by an initial training in philosophy and a European formation in Talmudic reading. Levinas' philosophical argument as a whole pre-

sents itself as one great phenomenological foundation and elaboration of a single proposition—namely, that the biblical command
"Thou shall not kill" is both the first word and the last word in metaphysics and in ethics, on the level of responsibility and on that of
justice, as ground of peace and of human rights.

A New Philosophy for Theology?
An Afterword by the Translator
Jeffrey Bloechl

Among those of us who seek an account of the status of contemporary rationality in the fate of the phenomenological movement, no small number have focussed attention on the manner in which some of its most prominent figures have insisted that rigorous thought requires a premise of fundamental "atheism." For Husserl, this was strictly a matter of remaining on course toward phenomenology's virtual goal of a form of reflection unimpeded by any qualification whatsoever, thus a form of reflection in which consciousness, once all data have been reduced from it, could appear as itself to itself. It is not evident that Husserl's "atheism" (agnosticism might be a better word) is much tempered by either his epistemological orientation or the serious difficulties awaiting the progress of his thinking. To the contrary, one need only observe that a truly "pure consciousness" neither *has* an object nor *is* an object in order to conclude that, whether or not actually achieved, the 'object' of transcendental phenomenology is in an important sense nothingness (cf. *Ideen. Erstes Buch* §58). Responding to Husserl, Heidegger also gives a certain nothingness a privileged place in phenomenology, but now as its buried source rather than its distant end. Heidegger focuses on Dasein's encounter with its own death, from which it realizes that it is first and foremost alone with itself. What is the content of this realization? Dasein will have heard the call of being, which is to say a call from beyond beings, hence the call of nothing. For Heidegger, the ultimate relation, the relation beyond beings and their meaning is the relation with being as nothingness. It is as that which stands on nothing and in nothing that Dasein is alone. In *Sein und Zeit*, methodological atheism (§7) discloses existential solipsism (§ 40). What began as an epistemological precaution has quickly yielded the basis for a new anthropology (Heidegger's aversion to this word notwithstanding). Philosophy has no need of God to understand who or what we are, and indeed must answer those questions as if God does not exist.

There are (and have been) at least three main ways to respond to this development in the name of religious transcendence: one can either (1) contest any number of its essential premises, (2) concede its legitimacy but parry its attempts to do more than expel religion from the precincts of philosophy, or (3) attempt to move through but also beyond the entire venture. This last procedure, perhaps because it alone brings something really new to philosophy after Heidegger, is currently most prominent. The father of this movement is, of course, Emmanuel Levinas. *Levinas*, who turned against Husserl and toward Heidegger already in 1929, but then away from Heidegger as well, and on this very question of religion, barely six years later, in his essay, "De l'Évasion." But also Levinas who described a stratum of life anterior to light or representation in some ways remarkably similar to the object of an entire series of dense works by Michel Henry; whose thought of primordial donation precedes that of Jean-Luc Marion by nearly two decades; and who finally clarified all of this with the notion, present in the work of Jean-Louis Chrétien, of an appeal understood only and already in the response (**AE** 190/149). None of this is to pretend that Henry, Marion, or Chrétien—all post-Heideggerian philosophers of religion, at least in part—are in essential agreement with Levinas. It is, however, to invoke the possibility that any movement through phenomenology and toward religion will be Levinasian, and in this particular respect: whether approached through life, donation, or a pure appeal, the religious relation excluded by phenomenology becomes thinkable again through a movement 'downward', anterior to the domain ruled by phenomenology. Levinas' critique of Heidegger presents itself as immanent, much in the style of Heidegger's own critique of Husserl. Refashioning the master's position from within, Levinas opens Heideggerian ontology to what it could never see: our relation to being is not the last word in human existence and experience. Nor is it the first.

The forms in which Levinas gives positive expression to this project have long since become familiar features of the contemporary philosophical landscape. According to *Totalité et Infini*, the face of the other person is the self-expression of an otherness which is literally absolute. The otherness of the other has always already withdrawn from the flesh in which it appears and the meaning I spontaneously assign to it. Already gone from the experience which registers it, it is also already out of reach of both light and logic. This includes the logic of negation, which is where Sartre would seem to have stopped. Against Sartre, Levinas asserts that the otherness of the other is surplus and excess, which furnishes the proper explanation of Levinas' notion that the human face is a "trace" of the other. It is also the essential link between these earlier thoughts centered on the encounter with the other person, and Levinas' later work on the subject who undergoes that experience. The reversal of intentionality indicated in a 'datum' striking from wholly beyond consciousness—*it* constitutes *me*: I am the one who receives it—necessarily implies a subject defined most profoundly by passivity. At least on this central point, *Otherwise than Being or Beyond Essence* remains closely in step with *Totalité et Infini*.

This very consistency or, if one does not accept it, the extremity of its separate theses, has focussed sharp and growing attention on the sparsity of Levinas' discussions of politics and morality, two areas from which one might well expect serious complications for his basic distinction between the otherness of the other person and the "sameness" of the one who encounters and responds to her. With regard to a phenomenology of that encounter, one misses, for instance, a clear distinction between an inter-cultural other and an intra-cultural other, a distinction noticeably suspended in Levinas' use of the single word "Stranger" for both meanings (**TI** 9/39 and 47/75). Can one hope to rehabilitate that difference without granting a necessary place for the politics of recognition? As for the infinite and unqualified responsibility which he correlates with welcoming an otherness beyond all identity, one wonders whether and how goodness can be concretely determined without the help of moral norms of any kind. Confronted by someone in need, must we—and can we—give up every divergence from direct and immediate care, every mediation or external definition of what constitutes a proper response?

In the absence of close attention to these questions, Levinas' work can indeed look like an all or nothing venture in which everything is staked on overcoming ontology as first philosophy, at the price of reducing not only that ontology, but also economics, politics, morality, and theology to inner functions of a life defined first and foremost by infinite responsibility. To be sure, Levinas' own major works, at least those which he characterizes as philosophical, seem to support this conclusion. Does not *Totalité et Infini* begin with a vigorous denunciation of "morality" and "politics"? Do we not find economics and theology pilloried wherever Levinas pauses to refer to them?

Morality and politics denounced? Yes, but perhaps only in so far as they pretend to primacy over the ethical-religious relation. Economics and theology pilloried? Again yes, but perhaps only pending their reconstruction in line with that same relation. With the exception of some extensive treatment of labor, possession, and habitation, mainly in *Totalité et Infini,* Levinas' major works offer only isolated cues to support such interpretations. A first important contribution of Roger Burggraeve's books lies here, in having assembled the numerous interviews and short essays in which Levinas turns out to have given considerable attention to these otherwise neglected themes. Beginning with an account of Levinas' own ontology (Chapter One) and the manner he redefines it in light of his description of the other person (Chapter Two), Burggraeve moves gradually into the relatively new territory of what his subtitle announces as a well developed viewpoint on peace and human rights (Chapter Three). Arriving then at Levinas' detailed and sometimes startling practical reflections (Chapter Four), one has the impression of having finally located the missing pieces of a picture long felt to be incomplete.

But perhaps these new pieces are more than additions to a work already framed and underway. The charge that Levinas' morality and politics are *ad hoc* ought to be dismissed at once. Responsibility, he tells us, is defined by one's relation to the other person here and now. Of course, were there only two of us in the world, my neighbor's call for help, interrupting my concern with my own needs, would divide my possible response evenly between caring only for myself and not her, or else caring only for her and not myself. This is Levinas' prototypical ethical situation, and it is understandable how, taken out of context, it has incurred furious resistance: were ethics solely a matter of the I-other relation, there could be nothing to distinguish the content of duty from immediate and total self-sacrifice. This, however, is for Levinas an imaginary danger, or perhaps the danger of the imaginary. The other person who faces me "is from the first the brother of all other men" (AE 201/158) so that that face must be considered not only unique in the singularity of its appeal here and now, but also universal in its essential reference to all those others who share the earth.

But the presence of the third person does more than save the life of the responsible subject. By calling to me with equal force but from a different position than the first person, the third person makes it necessary for me to compare the two appeals, thus to measure their distance and difference, deliberate over how to apportion my resources, and judge how much I can and should give to each. The imposition of limits on radical responsibility both saves the subject from its own responsibility and gives birth to what Levinas calls "justice." To be sure, this would be a justice and in turn a politics which are subordinate to ethics, but the fact remains that by not only formulating this possibility but also, as Burggraeve's work plainly demonstrates, applying it with appreciable precision, Levinas has furnished religious thought with one basis from which to intervene in the public sphere with a confidence rarely glimpsed since the French revolution.

Are the just act and political engagement then merely a concretization of radical responsibility? If Levinas' analysis of the third person does not arise *ad hoc*, is it then only an extrapolation of the dual ethical relation into the complex network of social relations? Before responding to these questions, Burggraeve would have us ask first how justice is even possible. If, as Levinas has argued, the movement of self-identification, out from oneself and back toward oneself, meets the other person before completing that return, then everything one is and does is already, in a fundamental sense, a response to that person. A good act is defined by accepting that responsibility and committing oneself to caring for one's neighbor. Rejecting or qualifying it defines evil. The just act will therefore be nourished first by the altruism of the good act, but divided as to how that goodness is to be focussed. This, in turn, means embracing habits and moral norms, entering society, and becoming a citizen. Justice, writes Levinas, can be established only if I, in the very radical responsibility which truly comprises me, can "become an other like the others" (AE 205/160-161).

The plurality of such others can not be the plurality of atomism, in which each of us would be *the same as* the others. Levinas' description of the human face has already ruled this out: the otherness of the other person is absolute; her identity, thus irreducible to anything I might make of it, is in that sense unique. Each such face confronts a subject with this sense of uniqueness: the other person looks from before and beyond any comparison or equation. It is this extreme uniqueness, interpreted by Levinas as an infinite otherness, which is revealed in every human face, so that as a general concept the face can be said to ground every relation and unite the whole of human society. Levinas describes a pluralism anterior to any totality. Referring to the way it is opened up by the self-withdrawal of infinity, he also calls it "creation." Creation is the ethical plurality of humans bound one to the other before or outside of any totality, thus where nothing mediates or intervenes. It is most deeply in this sense that each of us can be said to be responsible not only to the other person here and now, but also all the others, equally and at once.

If the response itself therefore opens immediately on to simultaneous relations with *all* the others, and not the single relation with this one person who faces me here and now, then the morality and politics which interrupts the exclusive, ethical relation can be considered to correct it. However, the final horizon of each act will remain that ethical relation, so that the true morality and politics will have been convoked by an appeal which they can never fully satisfy. Here Levinas' philosophy displays a combination of revolutionary impulse and extreme concretion more often associated with Marxism, a fact that no doubt explains the otherwise surprising interest in his work by liberation theologians such as Enrique Dussel and Juan Carlos Scannone: no system or institution is immune from a constant and, if necessary, radical critique wherever it treats people as numbers or examples rather than unique individuals.

One rightly objects that this way of filling responsibility out with justice seems to make it into a matter of conscience and thus the very sort of individual capacity that the ethics of the other person is clearly meant to overturn. Levinas addresses this point head on, immediately after his discussion of justice in *Otherwise than Being or Beyond Essence*. There, as in fact throughout his work, this difficulty is developed in terms of the relation between being, or individual existence, and responsibility for the other, or the advent of goodness. The act which starts from me or depends on me is always in danger of referring first or only to me, which for Levinas is also to impose limits on care for the other person. This ambiguity, inevitable and irreducible, is arguably the central concern of the ethical philosophy which, as any reader of Levinas knows, never tires of calling it to our attention (**AE** 209-210/164-165). The act which proceeds from conscience is a good act and not a selfish act only to the degree that it is nourished first by ethical insight. But even this is dangerous, or perhaps above all this: if the goodness of an act consists in its selfless devotion to the other person, then the good life consists in endless commitment to go beyond every reservation or hesitation limiting that devotion. This extraordinary effort, where responsibility permeates one's entire existence, threatens one with extreme exhaustion, and thus with collapse—a collapse going all the way to loss of one's very identity. After all, the life for the other has already suspended concern for oneself. Levinas calls the undefined void into which this exhausted individual sinks the *il y a*, or "there is." To live concertedly for the other is to take upon oneself the task of handing oneself over to the other, of dedicating one's own existence more and more to an insatiable appeal for help. But one must not forget that that existence is needed to serve the other, and indeed presupposed in the effort to do so. Existence must always come to the service of the responsibility which commands it from on high. This reminder, however, does not license a return to competing narcissisms. As Levinas has already said, the community of beings defined in advance by responsibility for the other is plural and in that sense fraternal, not atomistic and conflictual. Existence at the service of the other person can avoid de-personalization only if it recurs not to self-centeredness but justice, in which individual identity is conferred only in community.

Justice then is not only the domain of ethically-inspired social commitment, but also a name for authentic human being, as defined first by its relation to the other and not itself. And the self-with-drawal of infinity which yields ethical plurality both opens morality and politics to religion and keeps that religion beyond the reach of being. Ontology, in other words, is circumscribed by the ethico-religious philosophy which makes being oscillate with responsibility. In turn, Levinas' God beyond being would appear to be the linchpin for the return of the theologico-political *after Heidegger's unmasking of metaphysics as onto-theology*. This God is not a being, and ethical pluralism is not founded in it. We have long known that the philosophy of Levinas presents us with a God which is neither the God of the philosophers nor of the sociologists and philosophers of culture, a God which, as the likes of Lucien Goldmann and Marcel Gauchet have told us, human history no longer knows except in a tragic desire for what we already know is no longer possible. But as Burggraeve has established here, it nonetheless does manage to yield a positive theory of politics in which equality and human rights are assured by constant reference to an authority which can never be embodied by any single one of us. Still, Levinas' politics is not that of modern democracy, and the open space it turns around is not that of some-one like Claude Lefort, who centers modern democracy on the seat left empty after the death of the last French king who could claim to rule by divine right. Against Lefort, Levinas would argue that God does indeed have a place in the polis, and all the more since the seat long occupied by the false God, the God who lived and spoke through the king, has finally been vacated.

The critical import of Levinas' philosophy of religion for Christian fundamental theology has been noticed often enough, though rarely taken up. What has received far less attention, at least in English, are the points where that philosophy seems to rejoin Christian moral theology. Here again, Burggraeve's work has performed an important service. Students and adepts of proportionalism, for instance, will recognize in Levinas' description of the moment when conscience determines an act which serves one person but also deprives another a close approach to the moment where they would apply the principle of "proportionate reason" by which one seeks the act promising the most favorable proportion of good to evil. A more important example may well be what Levinas calls "small goodnesses" (Chapter

Four), which approximates what analytic ethicists might call "supererogation": an act, usually isolated and sudden, in which one serves or cares for an other in a manner going wholly beyond what is prescribed by duty, and in a situation where the attempt itself may appear hopeless. Here it is difficult not to think of *mercy* in hyperbolic form. For how to explain its excessive charity, except by the presence in us of something not only transcending nature, but also the moral law which rules it—in other words, as evidence of *grace*? To be sure, this calls for a great deal of scrutiny, since after all, Levinas' assertion that "ethics is the *only* element where religious transcendence can have meaning" (**NLT** 30, emphasis added) probably places him at odds with the predominant tendency of Christian thought, with its insistence on a ritual and indeed sacramental locus for religion. If there is to be a dialogue between Christian theology and Levinas' philosophy of religion, this would seem an excellent place to start, where a concept like grace, which has long tested the limits of metaphysical explanation, meets a new thinking attempting to redefine metaphysics itself.

Of course, the isolated moments of saintliness that Levinas associates with "small goodness" are not to be identified with the ever more disciplined acts of an individual committed to the goodness of being one-for-the-other person. One might rather say that Levinas has found in small goodnesses a phenomenon in which to substantiate the focus of his position as a whole. As those acts confirm, and indeed as Levinas always argues, ethics has to do with more than one's passions and the attempt to conform oneself to the law. Ethics attends not only to the selfish desires each of us pursues into and through social and moral limitations, but also to the desire which seems to escape that pursuit and transcend those limitations. This desire, plainly aiming beyond all objects, is rightly termed *religious*. It is also arguably the central concern of Levinas' philosophy as a whole. Perhaps this then tells us how to read his texts: the ethics of the other is intended as a transcendental analysis of human being which takes into account a dimension which can not be reduced to any form of self-interest. And while this does not seem to involve a claim that we can therefore suspend that self-interest definitively—Levinas' texts present themselves as prophetic, not utopian—it does include strong indications for how to improve our life in common.

INDEX OF NAMES AND SUBJECTS

Index

209

morality, 13, 165, 170, 195-196, 198, 200
Morocco, 25
mortal *pour soi*
mortality, 95, 114
Moscow, 26
Moses, 13, 22, 36, 118
Mosès, 13, 22, 36, 118
Mother Teresa, 182
murder, 6, 62-63, 95-96, 98, 158, 163
mystery, 90, 110, 117
mysticism, 68, 116, 159

narcissism, 43, 155
narcissistic
nation, 30, 59, 142-143
national egoism, 142-143
national socialism, 59-61, 81
national state, 73
nationalism, 81
natural, 28, 41, 43-44, 48, 56, 64, 66, 71, 141, 189
nature, 11, 29, 42-43, 55, 57, 60, 66, 69-70, 75, 81, 85, 93, 116-117, 120, 134, 140, 165-167, 201
Nazi, 27, 35, 68, 180
negation of negation, 96
neighbor, 18, 85, 103-105, 110, 135-136, 138-139, 142, 145-146, 150, 156, 160-162, 164, 178-179, 182-183, 185, 196-197
Nemo, 10, 37
neo-colonialism, 83
neo-Platonic, 74
Nietzsche, 120, 156
nihilism, 138
noetic totalization, 5-6, 53, 58, 91, 137
nomen actionis, 43
no-one, 47, 150
no-thing, 47, 150
nothingness, 47, 193

obedience, 56, 69, 74-75, 93, 186-187
Obernaï, 26
object, 22, 26, 54, 63-64, 86, 90, 98, 116, 134, 193-194
objectification, 64

objective, 24, 46, 50, 53-54, 73, 96, 125, 129-130, 133, 137, 152, 163, 165-167, 170, 173, 178-179
objectivity, 49, 111, 130, 157
October Revolution, 27
oeuvre, 37, 170
Of God Who Comes to the Idea
on n'est pas, on s'est, 48
One, 18, 21-24, 28-31, 33, 35-36, 38-39, 41-42, 44-45, 47-49, 52-53, 55-56, 58-83, 85-91, 93, 96-97, 99-107, 109-112, 114-116, 118-119, 121, 123-138, 140-143, 146-153, 155-164, 166-168, 170-172, 174, 176, 178, 181-184, 186-188, 190-191, 193-201
ontological, 31, 43, 45, 57, 60, 64, 68, 79, 171-172
ontology, 35, 60-61, 194, 196, 200
onto-theology, 200
opinion, 74, 186
Oran, 26
original freedom, 5, 47-48
orphan, 38, 94-95, 108, 119
Other, 5-7, 13-14, 17-19, 21, 28-29, 31, 33-36, 38-39, 41-44, 47-49, 51-60, 62-67, 69, 72-80, 82-83, 85-115, 117-121, 123-132, 134-136, 138-143, 145-148, 150, 152-158, 161, 164, 166, 168-171, 174-189, 195-201
Otherwise than Being, 9, 18, 117, 120-121, 195, 199

paradox, 13, 17, 49, 81, 112
pardon, 125
paresse, 49
Paris, 9-15, 21, 25-26, 32, 35-36, 39, 105, 152
Paris-Nanterre, 36
participation, 23, 47, 50, 60-61
particularism
peace, 3, 5-7, 13, 19, 41, 43, 45-47, 49, 51, 53, 55, 57, 59, 61, 63, 65, 67-75, 77, 79, 81, 83, 85-87, 89, 91, 93, 95, 97, 99-103, 105, 107, 109, 111, 113, 115, 117, 119, 121, 123, 125, 127, 129, 131, 133, 135-137, 139, 141,